# New Age Messiah Identified:

## Who Is Lord Maitreya?

Tara Center's "Mystery Man" Alive and Living in
London

Troy Lawrence

Huntington House Publishers

Unless otherwise indicated, Scripture quotations are from the King James Bible, © Thomas Nelson, Inc. 1976.

Huntington House Publishers

P.O. Box 53788

Lafayette, Louisiana 70505

Library of Congress Card Catalog Number 90-84093

ISBN 0-910311-17-X

Printed in the United States of America

# TABLE OF CONTENTS

# ACKNOWLEDGMENTS

I would like to thank the following individuals and organizations for making this book possible: Pat Matrisciana of Jeremiah Films, Dean Senti of Prophetic Insights, and most of all, I would like to thank my family for their patience and long-suffering as they supported me through this long and difficult period while researching and writing this book.

# INTRODUCTION

## Solving The Mystery

**M**y quest for the secret identity of Lord Maitreya has changed my life. It has convinced me that the Church will soon encounter severe affliction and hardship (unless the Christian community takes this warning seriously). Of the sixty journalists who began turning London upside-down to find this "New Age Messiah," only one other reporter came close to discovering him. His name is Jack Whitley. The paper trail left behind by Hollywood reporter Jack Whitley proved indispensable to me. Running into one dead end after another, however, Jack Whitley (like the other fifty-nine journalists) gave up his search.

Since I was a New Ager working for an important New Age organization during Jack's investigation, he will not recognize my pen name. Nevertheless, I must thank him publicly; for without his astute investigative work, I could have never discovered the true identity of the New Age Messiah, Lord Maitreya.

I must admit from the outset that I had one big advantage over Jack Whitley and the other journalists: I worked for one of the leading organizations of the New Age movement—the

Tara Center. I had access to files and secret memos that others—searching for Maitreya—could only dream about. But, being a faithful and devoted follower of the New Age movement, I would wait like everyone else for Maitreya to reveal himself on his "Day of Declaration."

I was going to wait like everyone else, that is, until something completely unexpected happened. Someone put in my hands a copy of a little book entitled *The Hidden Dangers of the Rainbow* by Constance Cumbey. This powerful book precipitated my conversion out of the New Age deception and into the light of Christianity.

Christianity! Most Christians are just not aware of the hatred and anger that word elicits in the hearts and minds of the New Age elite. After all, to a devoted New Ager, the Christian community is the last great hurdle between an old and decaying age of superstition and ignorance and a New Age of brotherhood, tolerance, and happiness for all—a hurdle that New Agers intend to overcome in a most brutal fashion.

A few days after my conversion, I decided to sever my ties with the Tara Center. It seemed only logical, now that I was a Christian, that I should quit before I was thrown out. As of yet, however, I had not revealed to anyone why I was quitting (probably more through fear than the leading of the Holy Spirit). I just wasn't looking forward to the ridicule and contempt I knew my friends would greet me with. I was prepared to endure this persecution, but only after reading my Bible enough to defend my faith through rational dialog. After all, I had a lot of friends and was highly respected in the organization.

## UNDERCOVER

Quitting the Tara Center gave me plenty of time to do some serious soul searching. Slowly, an idea began to take shape in my mind—An idea I, at first, rejected. "Why not," I thought to myself, "return to the Tara Center while concealing my Christianity." With God's help, I reasoned, I might be able to discover the man in whom millions are placing their trust for peace.

"Why not?—"I'll tell you why not," my better half warned, "because I am well aware of other ex-members of the New Age movement who have tried to divulge some of the plans being implemented by the New Age elite." Their untimely deaths seemed to me a most convincing reason to keep silent. Having prayed and languished over which path to take, however, I confidently presented myself to the Tara Center as a returned worker and heeded the advice of Shakespeare to "give every man thy ear but few thy voice." In short, I kept my Christianity to myself.

In my wildest dreams, I did not expect what happened next. I was allowed unsupervised access to the center's main computer! This kind of access was almost unheard of, and I attributed it to divine intervention. I was hardly able to contain my elation. I began going through mountains of files like a madman. After many months of research and plundering the voluminous documentation available to me, I began piecing the puzzle together.

But the paper trail was only the beginning. The trail led me from California to Karachi—from Pakistan to the inner chambers of the Ahmadiyya movement—from the Ahmadiyya movement to a small but powerful group called the "Hassasines." A group so dangerous we derive the term "assassin" from them.

My life has been threatened many times, I have been physically attacked, and I've even been the victim of a high-speed chase—all in the hope of silencing me. I have, however, never regretted my decision to go public (not even after I learned that fellow laborer Randall Baer had been mysteriously killed).

I eventually discovered that Maitreya is the leader of the Ahmadiyya movement in Islam. The Sufi movement alone contributes fifteen million followers in every Muslim nation to his worldwide network. This of course does not include the millions of New Agers who are ready to fall at his feet in America and other Western countries on his "Day of Declaration."

## NEW AGE AGENDA

It is surprising to me that most Christians are simply not aware of the high level of expectancy among New Agers concerning the appearance of this New Age Messiah. The Christian community in America seems to be almost oblivious to the tremendous amount of work and preparation occurring at this very moment. This preparation includes getting Americans psychologically and emotionally ready to embrace Maitreya when he declares himself.

For those of you who believe that New Agers are just harmless kooks, I beg you to reconsider. The New Agers are very strategically placed in key positions of authority. In business, education, and television, they have been enormously successful in effectuating change in America. In television alone, their successes have come not in small advances but in quantum leaps.

If you doubt that young minds are being predisposed to accepting this mystical Messiah, you need only turn on your TV set next Saturday morning. You will be deluged with New Age symbolism and occult imagery and doctrine: pyramidology, crystal power, ram-heads, serpents, magic . . . "Just a fad," you say. Hardly—I and many other dedicated New Agers worked tenaciously for years to bring about this kind of change. We coerced and cajoled and persuaded many executives in the major networks to embrace our hope and to help us spread our New Age gospel. We acquired friends in high places in both political and corporate America. And those who would not become our friends, we (with surprising success) often maneuvered out of office.

## THE PERSECUTION BEGINS

I cannot over emphasize that the greatest obstacle to ushering in the New Age is the Church. The seeds of hatred against Christians are already planted in subtle ways in textbooks across the nation but the real attack is scheduled for 1992-96. From subtle hint and insinuation to blatant accusation, the Christian community will be held responsible for everything from AIDS and anti-social behavior toward the homosexual community to world hunger.

The anger generated against the Church by the media will quickly turn into oppressive legislation that will tightly regulate the movement of the Church. Groups like 2 Live Crew will be free to spread their venom and create an environment in which women and children can't safely walk the streets, but the Christian community will have very few rights to free speech.

Lord Maitreya is indeed alive and well and living in London. I am not presumptuous enough to insist that he is the Antichrist. Although, there are many who believe that he is. That, I think, should be decided by minds much greater than mine. I am, however, certain that he is the one that millions of New Agers are preparing for. He is the great, great-grandson of Ghulam Ahmad and thus the 5th Khalifa of the Ahmadiyya movement. He waits only for the death of his uncle (who has no son) Tahir Ahmad, who is even now in ill health. To the Muslims he is the long awaited Imam Mahdi; to the Hindus he is Krishna; the Buddhists will accept him as there long awaited fifth Buddha; to the Jews he will be the hoped for Messiah. And to the unsuspecting Christian, he will be received as the returned Christ.

Lord Maitreya arrived in England from Pakistan a few years ago. He is now living in southeast London. He is at this time twenty-nine years old and was born in February 1962. Only his closest disciples know his true identity. The Maitreya mantle almost fell on him in 1982, but the time was not yet right as I will demonstrate in this book. His name and full identity are disclosed herein.

His hour, however, is rapidly approaching. The coalescing political, environmental, animal rights, and diverse array of movements will all avail themselves to him when he appears. He will need only to speak from the platform they have prepared. And what about the Judeo-Christian communities that resist his authority? Like Oscar Wilde's "Happy Prince," they will be thrown on the trash heap. I only ask that you read on and consider the evidence.

# REVIEW

On the 25th of April, 1982, full page advertisements were published in twenty of the world's major newspapers and in almost a dozen languages. The ads boldly proclaimed: "THE CHRIST IS NOW HERE." Many Christians then asked themselves: "Is the Antichrist Now Here?"

The ads were placed by the Tara Center—a New Age networking organization and press office for Benjamin Creme now known throughout the world as the New Age "John the Baptist." The ad declared that the Lord Maitreya was the Christ returned, and he would be appearing soon via worldwide radio and television broadcast called "The Day of Declaration."

I was, in 1982, a young Aquarian (New Ager) dedicated to helping Creme prepare the way for the "World Teacher." When Maitreya didn't show as scheduled (June '82), I did some hard soul-searching. I spent the next two full years studying the religions of the world and eventually became a born-again Christian in 1984. For the last several years, I have gone back into the movement—this time undercover—to expose the secret identity of Lord

Maitreya and to expose the real beliefs and goals of the occult hierarchy. This book is the culmination of that investigation.

Will you be prepared for the changes that will come in the next few years?

The advertisements placed by the New Age organization and press office for Benjamin Creme included the following:

*"The World Has Had Enough . . . Of Hunger, Injustice, War. In Answer To Our Call For Help, As World Teacher For All Humanity, THE CHRIST IS NOW HERE."*

(Benjamin Creme-*L.A. Times*: April 25, '82)

Jesus warned, "Wherefore if they shall say unto you, 'behold, he is in the desert'; go not forth; 'behold, he is in the secret chambers', believe it not" (Matt. 24:26).

Jesus warned that in the last days there shall arise many false Christ and false prophets, "For there shall arise false Christ, and false prophets, and shall shew great signs and wonders; insomuch that, if it were possible, they shall deceive the very elect" (Matt. 24:24).

This book is about a false Christ called Maitreya, and his forerunner: a false prophet by the name of Benjamin Creme. The words attributed to Creme at the head of this page are those that appeared as part of a full page advertisement. These ads appeared in April of 1982 in twenty major newspapers around the world. A few weeks after the ad, Benjamin Creme held a news conference at the Ambassador Hotel in Los Angeles, California. There he told journalists that soon the New Age "Messiah" would make himself known to the world. He said that Maitreya—the New Age "Christ"—was from a desert place in Pakistan, but he had taken up residence at a secret abode in London, England. He told us that Maitreya would appear to the world on his "Day of Declaration." On that day, he would appear on television via worldwide satellite hookup. Then, said Creme, the world would see him as their "Messiah." Since then, Creme has appeared on hundreds of radio and television programs around the globe: preparing the way for his "Lord Maitreya."

Many excellent books have been published in recent years dealing with Creme, Maitreya, and the New Age movement in general. These include *Hidden Dangers of the Rainbow* by Constance Cumbey, *Peace, Prosperity and the Coming Holocaust* by Dave Hunt, *Dark Secrets of the New Age* by Texe Marrs and, a decade earlier, *The Late Great Planet Earth* by Hal Lindsey. These books, and others, have documented the Luciferian roots and occult goals of the New Age movement. Those authors, and others, agree that the New Age movement, which I call Aquarianity, is the platform from which the end-time Antichrist shall arise. This book, *New Age Messiah Identified*, goes far beyond the others by revealing the secret identity of Maitreya. This book also exposes the false Aquarian propaganda and the hitherto secret plans of the occult hierarchy.

## *THE TARA CENTER AD*

Once you understand what progress Creme and the New Age organizations have made in the last few months, it will become quite clear why Creme should be taken very seriously in the 1990s.

Here is the full text of the ad from the Tara Center that appeared in April 1982:

THE WORLD HAS HAD ENOUGH . . . OF HUNGER, INJUSTICE, WAR. IN ANSWER TO OUR CALL FOR HELP, AS WORLD TEACHER FOR ALL HUMANITY . . .

### THE CHRIST IS NOW HERE
### HOW WILL WE RECOGNIZE HIM?

*Look for a modern man concerned with modern problems—political, economic, and social. Since July, 1977, the Christ has been emerging as a spokesman for a group or community in a well-known modern country. He is not a religious leader, but an educator in the broadest sense of the word—pointing the way out of the present crisis. We will recognize Him by His extraordinary spiritual potency, the universality of His viewpoint, and His love for all humanity. He comes not to judge but to aid and inspire.*

## WHO IS THE CHRIST?

*Throughout history, humanity's evolution has been guided by a group of enlightened men, the Masters of Wisdom. They have remained largely in the remote desert and mountain places of the earth, working through their disciples who live openly in the world. This message of the Christ's reappearance has been given primarily by such a disciple trained for his task for over 20 years. At the center of this "Spiritual Hierarchy" stands the World Teacher, Lord Maitreya, known by Christians as the Christ. And as Christians await the Second Coming, so the Jews await the messiah, the Buddhists the Fifth Buddha, the Moslems the lmam Mahdi, and the Hindus await Krishna. These are all names for one individual. His presence in the world guarantees there will be no third World War.*

## WHAT IS HE SAYING?

*"My task will be to show you how to live together peacefully as brothers. This is simpler than you imagine, My friends, for it requires only the acceptance of sharing. How can you be content with the modes within which you now live: when millions starve and die in squalor, when the rich parade their wealth before the poor; when each man is his neighbor's enemy; when no man trusts his brother? Allow me to show you the way forward into a simpler life where no man lacks; where no two days are alike; where the Job of Brotherhood manifests through all men. Take*

*your brother's need as the measure of your action and solve the problems of the world."*

## WHEN WILL WE SEE HIM

*He has not yet declared His true station, and His location is known to only a very few disciples. One of these has announced that soon the Christ will acknowledge His identity and within the next two months will speak to humanity through a worldwide television and radio broadcast. His message will be heard inwardly, telepathically, by all people in their own language. From that time, with His help, we will build a new world.*

## WITHOUT SHARING THERE CAN BE NO JUSTICE:

## WITHOUT JUSTICE THERE CAN BE NO PEACE:

## WITHOUT PEACE THERE CAN BE NO FUTURE

*This statement is appearing simultaneously in major cities of the world.*

What could possibly be wrong with such a message of peace? Nothing—unless the purpose of the message is to deceive. Jesus warned, "Beware of false prophets, which come to you in sheep's clothing, but inwardly they are ravening wolves" (Matt. 7:15). In this book we shall closely examine the above statements, and reveal the secret identity of Maitreya: the New Age "Messiah."

# 1

# PART ONE

## A Look At Several False Messiahs Throughout History

As any student of religious history knows, there have been many false Christ throughout the history of the world. Even in Jesus' own day, Judas of Galilee and Theudas led many in the Holy Land astray. After them came Simon Magus—the Magician who tried to purchase the power of God from the apostles. He went around after that claiming to be the Holy Spirit. Yet, there was nothing "holy" about him. The Sanhedrin, in Jesus' day, was so paranoid about false Messiahs running around wreaking havoc upon the land and people, that when the true Messiah appeared proclaiming his rightful place, they lumped him in with the false Christ. They delivered him over to the Romans to be crucified.

In my quest to discover the identity of Maitreya, the New Age "Messiah," I studied the histories and doctrines of many self-proclaimed "Christ" that have appeared over the last few thousand years. Why bother with them? Because just as Melchizedek, Moses, and Joshua, etc., were types of the true

Messiah that would come: Jesus of Nazareth; likewise, the false Messiahs are types of the coming ultimate false messiah: the Antichrist.

John the Beloved warned, "Little children, it is the last time: and ye have heard that Antichrist shall come, even now are there many Antichrists; whereby we know it is the last time" (1 John 2:18).

John seemed to be telling the saints that the Antichrists were types of the Antichrist to come. Jesus himself warned of false Christ to come:

> Then if any man shall say unto you, Lo, here is Christ, or there; believe it not. For there shall arise false Christ, and false prophets, and shall shew great signs and wonders; insomuch that, if it were possible, they shall deceive the very elect. (Matt. 24:23-24)

The Jews were expecting a Messiah to fulfill many specific prophecies. Jesus fulfilled these prophecies to the letter. Afterward, the scribes and religious doctors went to great pains to "explain away" all the prophecies concerning the Messiah, which Jesus had fulfilled. This left the door wide open for false Messiahs to plague the Jews for millennium to come. Why did the Jews try to deny these prophecies that had, before Christ, pointed to the Messiah, but since the coming of Jesus, "meant something else" entirely? Because the Christian missionaries were having so much success showing the common people that Jesus of Nazareth had fulfilled the messianic prophecies.

Not many years after the ascension of Christ, there came another claiming messiahship in Jerusalem. Since the scribes had busied themselves for the few decades past in explaining away many messianic prophecies, they really had no sure way to "check" the credentials of this new Messiah. This new Messiah's name was Simon Bar Koseva. He became famous as a Zealot leader rallying the Jews to throw off the heavy yoke of Rome by force of arms. His men began to call him Simon

Bar Kochba. They identified him with the prophecy of Balaam who saw "a Star (kokav) out of Jacob" that would rise and smite the enemies of Israel (Num. 24:17). Simon enjoyed his new title. He even had coins struck showing himself bearing a pot of manna and the rod of Aaron—both messianic symbols. The scribes loved Simon, and they were certain that he was their Messiah.

Yet, Simon began to act very unmessiah like—at least very unchristian like. He began to cut fingers off the hands of his men for the least infraction. The territory his brave soldiers won from the Romans, he declared, became his newly acquired private property.[1] Simon was even harsher on the Romans.

The Romans killed this "invincible Messiah" and perhaps half a million Jews that followed him. The Christian Jews had fled long before because Simon was killing them off—they didn't accept him as their Messiah. Simon so enraged the Romans that they destroyed Jerusalem and, for good measure, destroyed the temple there. They destroyed the temple so thoroughly that not one stone was left upon another.[2] If this sounds familiar, it's because Jesus prophesied of it decades before it happened: "And Jesus said unto them, 'See ye not all these things? Verily I say unto you, There shall not be left one stone standing upon another, that shall not be thrown down' " (Matt. 24:2).

The Romans put a quick end to the rebellion of the Jews but not to the false Messiahs. Moses of Crete soon came on the scene. He promised to part the Mediterranean Sea so that the Jews of Crete could pass through it with him to the Holy Land where Moses would rule with power and great glory. Moses stood upon a rock at the shore, waved his hands, said some inspiring words, and bade his followers to cast themselves a highway in the sea and march to the Holy Land. Within minutes, hundreds of the faithful drowned. Those left were crying for revenge, but Moses was nowhere to be found.[3]

In the eighth century came Serene of Syria, a Jew who tried to rally the Jews to drive the Muhammadans from the Holy Land. The only person driven from the Holy Land that year was Serene. Four hundred years later, in Persia, David Alroy declared himself the Messiah and summoned the Jews to rebel against the Muslims by killing them. The only person killed in that rebellion was David. Three hundred years after that Solomon Molcho gained large audiences as the Messiah of the Jews. The Inquisition gave him his largest audience of all when they burned him at the stake.

Other false Christ came and went among the Jews, such as Sabbatai Sevi. This man Sevi claimed to be the long awaited Messiah. He travelled extensively. Here is an example of an epistle he wrote to his followers:

> The only, and first-born Son of God, Sabbatai Sevi, the Messiah and Saviour of Israel, to all the Sons of Israel, peace. Since that you are made worthy to see that great Day of Deliverance and Salvation unto Israel, and Accomplishment of the Word of God, Promised by his Prophets, and our forefathers, and by his beloved Son of Israel: let your bitter sorrows be turned into Joy and your Fasts into festivals, for you shall weep no more, sons of Israel, for God having given you this unspeakable comfort rejoice with Drums, Organs, and Music, giving thanks to Him for performing His promise from all Ages.[4]

Nathan (Sevi's prophet) rallied the scribes to write declarations promoting Sevi.[5] His popularity among Jews was enormous, and the Christians of the day either admired or feared him. Sevi was very confidant that he could lead the Jews back to Jerusalem and proclaim himself king. Since the Muslims controlled the Holy Land, Sevi decided to travel to the capital of the Muslim empire. Sevi wrote several letters along the way, prophesying great events, and signing the letters as follows:

The man who is the Divine Messiah,
mighty as a lion, strong as a bear, the Lord's
anointed.[6] The Messiah of the God of Jacob,
the Heavenly Lion, King of Justice, the King
of Kings.[7]

Indeed, Sevi had impressed and awed even the Christian
royalty of Europe, but the sultan of Istanbul was not ready to
be as impressed. Sevi came to him proclaiming himself the
Messiah and King of the Jews. Sevi demanded that he be
given the Holy Land as an eternal possession. If the sultan
hindered him in any way, Sevi warned, God would destroy
him.

The sultan decided to call his bluff. He had Sevi placed
against a wall and ordered a hundred archers to aim for his
chest. "Submit to Allah and His Prophet or die!" (i.e., become
a Muslim) he told Sevi. Suddenly, Sevi received a "revelation," changed his name to a good Muslim one, and practiced
the Muslim faith until his death. The sultan renamed him
Mehmed Effendi, and made Sevi his official doorkeeper. This
devastated Sevi's followers. They convinced themselves that
God was punishing them by sending false Messiahs because
they weren't keeping the Law of Moses well enough. Thus,
the great Talmudic and Haggidic period commenced. Their
great era of "Messiahs" had ended.

There were more false "Christian" Messiahs through the
years than Jewish Messiahs. One of the most famous, or shall
we say "infamous," was Thomas Muntzer.

Thomas claimed to be the returning "Son of Man." Not
everyone agreed with him, however, he gained a large following. Muntzer proclaimed himself "Messiah" and bade his
followers to "go into battle" against the unbelievers. He told
his flock: "It is the battle. At them! At them! I will catch their
cannonballs in my sleeves!"[8] The cannon balls slaughtered
thousands of his followers. They found Thomas much later
hiding in a cellar; they beheaded him.[9]

Jan Matthyson came soon after Thomas. He claimed to be the "Son of David" and other glorious titles. Matthyson promised the peasants of Germany that he would build for them a New Jerusalem. The prince of the city he had donned "New Zion" had other ideas, however, and had his head cut off and put on a spike. Jan Bockelson immediately took his place as the "Promised One," saying that God had raised him up to be greater than Matthyson. He remarked, "Jan Bockelson of Leydon, the saint and prophet of God, must be king of the whole earth. His authority will extend over emperors, kings, princes, and all the powers of the world, and none shall rise above him. He will occupy the throne of his father, David and will carry the scepter till the Lord reclaims it from him."[10]

Many people gathered to this new Messiah, and they formed their "New Zion" in a town called Munster. Bockelson promised a paradise on earth. He created a paradise for himself but a hell for everyone else. Bockelson dressed in fabulous clothes; he dined on the finest foods; he surrounded himself with a harem of the most beautiful wives and daughters of Munster. He bade his followers to close the city to non-believers, and to defend it (i.e., him) to the end. Bockelson had promised that the time was soon coming in which they would be whisked to heaven, and that they should close themselves off from the outside. Bockelson was living like a king, but his faithful had a somewhat lower standard of living. One historian writes of their plight: "Terrible maladies, the consequences of famine aggravated the position of the inhabitants of the town; their flesh decomposed, they rotted living, their skin became livid, their lips retreated; their eyes, fixed and found, seemed ready to start out of their orbits; they wandered about, haggard, hideous, like mummies, and died by the hundreds in the street.[11]

Eventually the authorities raided Munster. Bockelson charged that they had no authority over him because he was "called by God and His Prophets." They took Bockelson and roasted him alive.[12]

In Russia, in the middle 1600s, came Daniel Philipovitch who declared, "I am the God announced by the prophets, come down to earth the second time for the salvation of the human race." His sect, called the Khylsti, died when he did. In 1770, in Russia, Kondrati Selivanov declared himself God and said that all men who would follow him into Paradise must be castrated, and that after their numbers reached 144,000, Christ would return. His sect, the Skoptsy, died out for two reasons; 1) Selivanov couldn't find 144,000 Russian men willing to be castrated, and 2) those that did couldn't leave any posterity to carry on the work.[13]

Also in the 1700s came James Nayler, an early Quaker leader who claimed to be Christ returned. When he rode into Bristol, England, shouts of "Holy, holy, holy, Lord God of Israel!" greeted him. The authorities convicted Nayler of blasphemy; they bore his tongue through with a red-hot iron and then branded a large "B" (for blasphemer) on his forehead. Nayler, after reconsidering his claim of messiahship, was set free.[14]

In America, in the late 1700s, several women, strangely enough, began to claim Messiahship. In the 1770s Mother Ann Lee proclaimed herself the "Female Principle of Christ" (Jesus being the "Male Principle"), and the "Redeemer of the race of man." She promised her disciples that if they would do a sacred dance, and live in strict chastity, they would become immortal like her. The sect was as "immortal" as she was.[15]

In the 1780s, came Jemima Wilkinson-the "Universal Friend." She established a commune to await the Lord's return in 1786. She instructed her followers that if she died before the Lord comes, her body should not be buried. The Lord, she said, would come to raise her up as he did the "sleeping" young woman mentioned in the Gospels. After waiting as long as they could, her disciples decided they "had" to bury her and let the Lord raise her as he did Lazarus.[16]

The Muslims had a long list of false Messiahs as well. The most colorful among them was "The Yemen Messiah." So great was his fame that the Caliph summoned him. The Caliph questioned the Yemen Messiah about his claims. "A sign," the Caliph said, "Give me a sign." The Yemen Messiah looked at the Caliph boldly and said "Cut off my head, and I will return to life again. There can be no greater sign than that." The Caliph replied, "If you can do that, all the world will believe you, including myself." The Caliph swiftly ordered the beheading of the Yemen Messiah, and that was that. Obviously, somebody got too over confident, or perhaps the Yemem Messiah was hoping that the Caliph would be so awe struck by the request that he would have "believed" without the "sign."[17]

Myriads of other false Christ—Jew, Christian, and Muslim—came through the years. Why did they come? Usually for power and money. Fifty years ago, in this country, came "Father Divine." He originally called himself "Father Devine," but one of his worshippers informed "God" that "divine" was spelled with an *i* and not an *e*. He proved to be as immortal as the others.

The most infamous of Father Divine's indirect disciples was "Reverend" Jim Jones. He needs no introduction. Promising his followers peace, prosperity, and happiness, if they worshipped only him, he gave his followers what many of these false Christ have given their followers. One former member of the People's Temple wrote about her experience:

> Most people think they're immune to brainwashing. They think they're too stubborn or too smart; their IQ is too high to be brainwashed.

> Jim Jones, however, changed our whole outlook and belief system very subtly. He got us to question the Bible. Then he pointed out the hypocrisy of Christian leaders who weren't living what they preached.

Step by step we found ourselves seduced more and more as Jim Jones undermined everything we'd held sacred, and gradually replaced what we had once believed with Marxist philosophy.

Soon we didn't want to wait for golden slippers and golden streets. We were going to build our own Utopia here and now. And we would do it through Marxism, because God didn't exist for us anymore.

The process was gradual, almost imperceptible, until the time came when we found ourselves swearing to do things we would never have thought we were capable of doing.

I don't believe I could actually have killed anyone, yet I signed an affidavit saying I would kill, destroy, or commit any act necessary to establish communist rule under Jim Jones.[18]

In recent years the false Messiahs have hit the news media again. The Rev. Sun Myung Moon came to this country from Korea a few years back. He claims to be the "Lord of the Second Advent," to finish the job Jesus "failed" to do. He created a stir, but until just recently, he was stirring around a federal prison cell for tax evasion.

The Bhagwan Shree Rajneesh startled Americans with his admonitions of free love and his eighty or so Rolls Royces. Christian cult watchers began to warn people of the probable danger of his teachings, but for the most part, (the secular media and others) labelled them "witch-hunters" and ignored them. No one ignored them, though, when the Bhagwan's disciples divulged that he had planned a mass poisoning of thousands of innocent people—a warning to anyone who would dare question the authority of the Bhagwan. Dan R. Schlesinger, one such Christian cult-watcher, reports on what happened to one disciple: "Ma Anand Sheela, former secretary to Indian guru Bhagwan Shree Rajneesh. She was sentenced to two twenty year prison terms after pleading guilty to eight federal and state charges. The court fined Sheela $400,000 and ordered her to pay $69,000 restitution for damages resulting from a January 15, 1985, fire she ordered to be set at the Wasco County (Oregon) Planning Office. Included among the charges: tampering with consumer products that poisoned more than 750 people; conspiracy to illegally intercept communications, which included a wire tapping; attempted murder; immigration fraud; and assaults in the first and second degrees for poisoning two Wasco County officials."

Yes, many false Christ have come and gone throughout the centuries. Their fruits are always bad! But, compared with the Antichrist, they are relatively harmless. Why? Because the coming Antichrist is not just a wicked man. He is a satanically inspired leader who will come with superior knowledge, working *real* miracles and deceiving, if it were possible, the very elect! Who is he, and what must Christians do to prepare for the tribulation to come? For these answers I turned to the Bible.

## THE MAN OF SIN REVEALED

I soon discovered that my quest for the identity of the "Man of Sin" was not going to be an easy one. I read dozens of commentaries hoping to learn something. They were almost all hopelessly divided on who it was, is, or will be. Hebrew Christian writer, Clifford Goldstein, found the same problem when he wrote on the Antichrist:

> Ever since the apostle John wrote that "Antichrist shall come" (1 John 2:18), Christians have speculated about his identity. The early church thought it was the Romans. The medievals feared that Antichrist was the Hussites, the Wycliffites, the Ottoman Turks, or the Jews. Luther and the Protestant Reformers named papal Rome as Antichrist. Spanish Jesuit Francisco Ribera rid papal

Rome of the stigma by identifying Antichrist as a still unknown end-time personage or power, a scenario bought by today's evangelical world. Current speculations about Antichrist encompass Henry Kissenger, secular humanism, Communism, the Trilateral Commission, the Illuminati, Guru Maharaj Ji, Germany, Ronald Reagan, the European Common Market, and even a computer in Belgium.[19]

Goldstein forgot to mention some of the other "candidates" for the job, here are a few that have been "selected" over the years:

Adolf Hitler

Attila the Hun

Frederick the Great of Germany

Napoleon

King Juan Carlos of Spain

Aleister Crowley

Nero

Caligula

Domitian

Muhammad

Ghengis Khan

Ummay Caliphs

Mussolini

Mikhail Gorbachev

President Sadat of Egypt

Joseph Stalin

The Popes

Martin Luther

Instead of picking one of the above, I decided to ask myself this question: "Who did John have in mind when he wrote the book of Revelation?" I thought, "Would John write to the early Christians, warning them of Antichrist, if such a person wouldn't show perhaps for hundreds or thousands of years?" Could John have been speaking about a man who lived in his day and would return again in these last days. Or, to say it another way, could it be that the spirit of Antichrist possessed someone in that day, and that same spirit would possess someone in this day. What about all the prophecies concerning the rise of the Antichrist, and his false prophet, in the last days? This was a dilemma for me.

Then I remembered that the Jews believed in only one coming of the Messiah. Yet, the prophecies speak of two separate advents. Jesus came once to Palestine, and he will come again in power and great glory to Jerusalem, just when, no one knows. I thought, "Could the same be true for the Antichrist?" After all, God cast Satan out of heaven because he wanted to be God (Isa. 14). God sent his son Jesus to be the Messiah and redeemer of the world. In dark imitation, Lucifer sent his "Christ" to the world as well. If God will send the true Christ twice—once two thousand years ago and again at the last day, then could it be that Satan will do the same for his "Christ."

Where should I begin to look? I had studied occultism pretty extensively as a Theosophist, and after I became a Christian, I studied the religions of the world. If this "Man of Sin" had appeared two thousand years ago, about the same time as Jesus, somewhere in the world occultists would have fond memory of him. I thought I already knew such an individual. Such a man could truly be said to be the "exact opposite" of Jesus. He was born the very same year as Jesus, but his life was just the opposite. Was he the one? I didn't know. I needed to go back to the Bible and list the "qualifiers" for the Antichrist.

Creme says that the Antichrist has come and gone; that it was not a man, but the "destructive force" of God. We can agree that Antichrist is the "destructive force" of Creme's god. Yet, Scripture clearly teaches that he is also a man:

Now we beseech you, brethren, by the coming of our Lord Jesus Christ, and by our gathering together unto him,That ye be not soon shaken in mind, or be troubled, neither by spirit, nor by word, nor by letter as from us, as that the day of Christ is at hand.

Let no man deceive you by any means; for that day shall not come, except there come a falling away first, and that man of sin be revealed, the son of perdition. (2 Thess. 2:1-3)

## PROPHECIES CONCERNING THE TRUE CHRIST

Before I could begin to understand biblical prophecies regarding the Antichrist, I needed first to understand biblical prophecies concerning the true Christ: Jesus of Nazareth. I found that Jesus fulfilled literally hundreds of prophecies concerning the coming Messiah. Here are just a few of them in their prophecy and fulfillment.

* Messiah shall be born of a woman (Gen. 3:15).
* Jesus was born of a woman (Matt. 1:20, Gal. 4:4).
* Messiah shall be born of a virgin (Isa. 7:14).
* Jesus' mother, Mary, was a virgin when she gave birth (Matt. 1:18-25).
* Messiah shall be the Son of God (Ps. 2:7). Jesus was the Son of God (Matt. 3:17).
* Messiah will be a descendant of Abraham (Gen. 22:18). Jesus was a descendant of Abraham (Matt. 11).
* Messiah shall be a descendant of Isaac (Gen. 21:12). Jesus was a descendant of Isaac (Matt. 1:2).
* Messiah would be a descendant of Jacob (Num. 24:17). Jesus was a descendant of Jacob (Matt. 1:2).
* Messiah shall be of the tribe of Judah (Gen. 49:10). Jesus was of the tribe of Judah (Heb. 7:14).

· Messiah shall be a descendant of Jesse (Isa. 11:1). Jesus was a descendant of Jesse (Matt. 1:6).

· Messiah shall be of the House of David (Jer. 23:5). Jesus was of the House of David (Mark 9:10).

· Messiah shall be born in Bethlehem (Mic. 5:2). Jesus was born in Bethlehem (Matt. 2:1).

· Wise men shall offer gifts to Messiah (Ps. 72:10). Wise men offered the child Jesus gifts (Matt. 2:1,11).

· Evil men shall massacre children trying to kill Messiah (Jer. 31:15). The evil king Herod massacred children trying to kill Jesus (Matt. 2:16).

· Messiah shall be called Immanuel (Is. 7:14). The Scripture calls Jesus Immanuel (Matt. 1:23).

· Messiah shall be a prophet (Deut. 18:18). The Scriptures call Jesus a prophet (Matt. 21:11).

· Messiah shall be a priest after the order of Melchizedek (Ps. 110:4). The Scriptures call Jesus a priest after the order of Melchizedek (Heb. 5:5-6).

· Messiah shall be a judge (Isa. 33:22). St. John calls Jesus a Judge (John 5:30).

· Messiah shall be a king (Ps. 2:6). The Bible calls Jesus a king (John 18:33-38).

· Messiah shall be anointed by the Holy Spirit (Isa. 11:2). The Holy Spirit anointed Jesus (Matt. 3:16-17).

· A messenger shall prepare the way for the Messiah (Isa. 40:3). John the Baptist prepared the way for Jesus (Matt. 3:12).

· Messiah shall first minister in Galilee (Isa. 9:1). Jesus first ministered in Galilee (Matt. 4:12-17).

· Messiah shall perform many miracles (Isa. 35:5). Jesus performed many miracles (Matt. 9:35).

· Messiah shall teach by Parables (Ps. 78:2). Jesus taught by parables (Matt. 13:34).

· Messiah shall come to the Temple (Mal. 3:1). Jesus came to the Temple (Matt. 21:12).

· Messiah shall enter Jerusalem riding upon a donkey (Zech. 9:9). Jesus entered Jerusalem riding upon a donkey (Luke 19: 35-37).

· Messiah shall be a "stone of stumbling" to the Jews (Ps. 118:22). Jesus was a "stone of stumbling" to the Jews (1 Pet. 2:7).

· Messiah shall be a "Light" unto the Gentiles (Isa. 60:3). Jesus was a "Light" unto the Gentiles (Acts 13:47-48).

· Messiah shall die but be resurrected (Ps. 16:10). Jesus died on the Cross but rose again (Luke 24:46).

· Messiah shall ascend to heaven (Ps. 68:18). Jesus, after his resurrection, ascended to heaven (Acts 1:9).

· Messiah shall be seated at the right hand of God (Ps. 110:1). Jesus sits at the right hand of God (Heb. 1:3).

· Messiah shall be betrayed by a friend (Ps. 41:9). A friend betrayed Jesus (Matt. 10:4).

· Messiah shall be betrayed for thirty pieces of silver (Zech. 11:12). Judas betrayed Jesus for thirty pieces of silver (Matt. 26:15).

· Messiah's "blood money" shall be thrown into God's house (Zech. 11:13). Jesus' "blood money" was thrown into the Temple (Matt. 27:5).

· Messiah shall be forsaken by his disciples (Zech. 13:7). His disciples forsook him (Mark 14:50).

· Messiah shall be accused by false witnesses (Ps. 35:11). False witnesses accused Jesus (Matt. 26:59-61).

· Messiah shall remain silent before his accusers (Isa. 53:7). Jesus remained silent before his accusers (Matt. 27:12-19).

- Messiah shall remain silent before his accusers (Isa. 53:7). Jesus remained silent before his accusers (Matt. 27:12-19).
- Messiah shall be wounded and bruised (Isa. 53:5). The soldiers wounded and bruised Jesus (Matt. 27:26).
- Messiah shall be smitten and spit upon ( Isa. 50:6). Jesus was smitten and spit upon (Matt. 26:67).
- Messiah shall be mocked (Ps. 22:7-8). The crowds mocked Jesus (Matt. 27:31).
- Messiah shall have his hands and feet pierced (Ps. 109:24). Jesus had His hands and feet pierced by crucifixion (Luke 23:33).
- Messiah shall die among criminals (Isa. 53:12). Jesus died among thieves (Matt. 27:38).
- Messiah shall be rejected by his people (Isa. 53:3). His people rejected him(John 7:5,48).
- Messiah shall be hated without a cause (Ps. 69:4). Religious leaders hated Jesus without a cause (John 15:25).
- Messiah's friends shall stand afar off (Ps. 38:11). Jesus' friends, at his death, stood afar off (Luke 23:49).
- At Messiah's death, people shall wag their heads (Ps. 109:25).
- At Jesus' death, people wagged their heads (Matt. 27:39).
- Messiah's garments will be parted, and lots cast for them (Ps. 22:18). The soldier cast lots for his garments (John 19:23 24).
- Messiah shall be offered gall and vinegar before his death (Ps. 69:21).
- Jesus was offered gall and vinegar right before his death (Matt. 27:34).

· Messiah, at his death, shall cry out that God has forsaken him (Ps. 22:1).

· Jesus cried out, right before his death, that God had forsaken him (Matt. 27:46).

· Messiah's bones shall not be broken (Ps. 34:20). The soldiers did not break his bones at his crucifixion (John 19:33).

· At Messiah's death, there shall be darkness over the land (Amos 8:9). At Jesus' death, there came darkness over the land (Matt. 27:45).

· Messiah shall be buried in a rich man's tomb (Isa. 53:9). His followers buried him in a rich man's tomb (Matt. 27:57-60).

## PROPHECIES CONCERNING THE ANTICHRIST

While the prophecies concerning the true Christ were many, the prophecies concerning the Antichrist were neither numerous nor obvious. I began to read various books by Christian authors on the Antichrist and biblical prophecy to try to piece together a group of prophecies that everyone, or most, agreed on. Finally, I could put a small, but workable, list together. Just about all the scholars I asked, and the books I had read, applied these Scriptures to the Antichrist. Here they are:

· He shall be named Apollyon (Rev. 9:11).

· He shall be from Asia Minor (Rev. 2:13).

· He shall have no desire for women (Dan. 11:37).

· He shall cause fire, or lightning to come down from heaven, and will perform satanic miracles (Rev. 13:13; Luke 10:18).

· He shall be worshipped as God, in the Temple of God (2 Thess. 2:4).

· The number of his name shall be 666 (Rev. 13:8).

After I had reviewed these prophecies, like a bolt of lightening striking me, I knew who this man of sin was.

Having studied many years deep into the occult, it was easy for me to piece these things together. Why? We must remember that John the Revelator was writing to Christians living in a pagan/occult world. Images, phrases, terms, and symbols he used to communicate to them were well known then—not so today. However, in the occult world, they are well known—then and now.

Who is he? Occult authorities tell uninitiated (new converts) New Agers that all the religious reformers throughout the ages were equal manifestations of the same "Force" called God. Jesus was just "one" among many avatars (incarnations of God) that came along for the betterment of man. Initiated New Agers know something different. They believe that Vishnu, the second person of the Hindu Trinity, has reincarnated into nine manifestations: Krishna and Buddha being the 8th and 9th respectively. The initiated look at Jesus as, at best, a minor avatar of a minor Hindu deity. Kalki is the name of the tenth, final and greatest, avatar of Vishnu. Even most Hindus believe that Kalki has not yet come, but the initiated know better!

The initiated believe that this present age is the Kaliyuga (Dark Age), and that Kalki must come and destroy this present creation, and create anew. The initiated believe that they will become the new Masters in the next creation. Why will Kalki come to destroy? Because this creation is degenerating. Only by death and destruction can the divine cycle be renewed: creation, preservation, destruction. In Sanskrit, the sacred tongue of the Hindus, "Kalki" means The Destroyer.

The initiated know that Kalki has come and gone already. They believe, however, that he will come again. Christians believe that Jesus will come again, a second time. Luciferians believe that Kalki has come, but will return in these last days. Who is he? That has been an occult secret for two thousand years.

The man initiated occultists revere as Kalki, the tenth and final avatar of Vishnu, is the personage known as

Apollonius of Tyana. This is a great secret known only to a select few! Does he fit the prophecies concerning the Antichrist? Let's see.

I will discuss first, his name: According to John's revelation, the fifth angel sounded, and a star fell from heaven. He was given the key to the bottomless pit. Out of the pit arose smoke, and out of the smoke came locusts. The locusts "had a king over them, which is the angel of the bottomless pit, whose name in the Hebrew tongue is Abaddon, but in the Greek tongue hath his name Apollyon" (Rev. 9:11). I checked Greek New Testament Lexicons. What does Apollyon mean? The same as it does in Hebrew: *The Destroyer*. Here are a few Christian scholars commenting on the name:

*Prof. Joseph A. Seiss:*

>   This king has a descriptive name. It is given in Hebrew and in Greek, showing that this administration has to do with Jews and Gentiles. Christ is named *Jesus* because He is *the Saviour*. This king is named *Abaddon* in Hebrew, and *Apollyon* in Greek, because he is *a* destroyer-the opposite of saviour.[20]

*Rev. Martin Kiddle:*

>   But why should John trouble to give the angel's name, in both *Hebrew* and *Greek*? ... Some have suggested that John was making a gibe against the heathen god Apollo, whom the pagan world venerated, and one of whose symbols was a locust.[21]

*Prof. Isbon T. Beckwith:*

>   The Apocalyptist gives the name to the angel of hell and translates it into Greek by *Apollyon, Destroyer*... Some find in the name Apollyon an indirect allusion also to the god Apollo, one of whose symbols was the locust and to whom plagues and destruction were in some cases attributed.[22]

*Prof. Thomas S. Kepler:*

> Apollo, son of Zeus, with its shrine. 'Son of God'—Apollo, the chief deity of Thyatira, Son of Zeus, is not to be the 'Son of God' for Christians; Jesus is the true 'Son of God.'[23]

In Paganism, the god Apollo could transform himself into different shapes. "The god Apollo was a solar king in heaven during the day, and a Lord of Death in the underworld at night," according to New Age propagandist Barbara Walker.

> His latter form became the Jewish Apollyon, Spirit of the Pit (Rev. 9:11). Apollo-Python was the *serpent* deity in the pit of the Delphic oracle, who inspired the seers with mystic vapor from his nether world. The Greek word for the pit was *[A]baton*, which the Jews corrupted into Abaddon—later a familiar Christian synonym for hell.

> Also called a *mundus* or earth-womb, the *[a]baton* was a real pit, standard equipment in a pagan temple. Those who entered it to "incubate" or to sleep overnight in magical imitation of the incubatory sleep in the womb, were thought to be visited by an "incubus" or spirit... Novice priests went down into the pit for longer periods of incubation, pantomiming death, burial, and rebirth from the womb of Mother Earth.[24]

The Bible tells us that Satan transformed himself into a serpent. Apollonius of Tyana claimed to be the 'son of Zeus'. Let us learn more about him.

## APOLLONIUS OF TYANA

The man known as Apollonius of Tyana was born in Tyana, in Cappodocia, Asia Minor (now Turkey), in the very same year that Jesus was born. His biographer was one Flavius Philostratus, a Roman historian. He travelled extensively throughout the known world, but he kept

Pergamos as his home base. Prof. F. C. Conybeare translated Philostratus' *The Life of Apollonius of Tyana* into English. Here he comments on the life of this man:

> The story of the life of Apollonius as narrated by Philostratus is briefly as follows. "He was born toward the beginning of the Christian era at Tyana, in Cappodocia, and his birth was attended according to popular tradition with miracles and portents. At the age of sixteen he set himself to observe in the most rigid fashion the almost monastic rule ascribed to Pythagoras, renouncing wine, rejecting the married estate, refusing to eat any sort of flesh... Apollonius went without shoes or wore only shoes of bark, he allowed his hair to grow long, and never let a razor touch his chin, and he took care to wear on his person nothing but linen, for it was accounted by him, as by Brahmans, an impurity to allow any dress made of the skin of dead animals to touch the person.
>
> "Before long he set himself up as a reformer, and betaking himself to the town of Aegae, he took up his abode in the temple of Aesculapius, where he rapidly acquired such a reputation for sanctity that sick people flocked to him asking him to heal them... He then set himself to spend five years in complete silence, traversing, it seems, Asia Minor, in all directions, but never opening his lips..."

If we may believe his biographer, he professed to know all languages without ever having learned them, to know the inmost thoughts of men, to understand the language of birds and animals, and to have the power to predict the future. He also remembered his former incarnation, for he shared the Pythagorean belief of the migrations of human souls from "body to body. . . . He visited Persia and India, where he consorted with the Brahmans. . . . He visited the cataracts of the Nile . . . [and] held long conversations with Espasian and Titus soon after the siege and capture of Jerusalem by the latter. . ."

Toward the end of the third century when the struggle between Christianity and decadent paganism had reached its last and bitterest stage, it occurred to some of the enemies of the new religion to set up Apollonius, to whom temples and shrines had been erected in various parts of Asia Minor, as a rival to the founder of Christianity. The many miracles that were recorded of Apollonius, and in particular his eminent power over evil spirits or demons, made him a formidable rival in the minds of pagans to Jesus Christ.[25]

Philostratus goes on to tell the story of Apollonius. He tells of his birth, life, many travels, and "resurrection" from the dead. We shall delve deep into the life and teachings of Apollonius in the third volume of The Last Days Trilogy: *Apocalyse Unsealed*. For our present purposes, however, let us see if the major events in his life "qualify" him as the man of sin.

## *HE SHALL BE CALLED APOLLYON*

Apollonius is the Latinized version of the Greek name Apollyon, which is a short form of the name Apollo-Python. Apollonius dressed like a Brahmin (a Hindu Aryan), spoke like a Brahmin, and acted like a Brahmin. When he visited India, the *Masters* summoned him. I discuss the Masters elsewhere in this volume. (They are demon entities that communicate to the Brahmins.) Could it be that they saw him as Kalki, the tenth and last incarnation of Vishnu? The named means *Destroyer*. Once in India, Philostratus writes, a Brahmin came to Apollonius and his travelling party and said: "Your party must halt here, but you must come on just as you are, for the Masters themselves issue this command." Philostratus comments: ·"The word *Masters* at once had a Pythagorean ring for the ears of Apollonius and he gladly followed the messenger."[26] It is interesting to note here that

John says his "name in the Hebrew tongue is Abaddon, but in the Greek tongue hath his name Apollyon" (Rev. 9:11).

## HE SHALL BE FROM ASIA MINOR

To the church at Pergamos in Asia Minor, John quoted Jesus, "I know thy works, and where thou dwellest, even where Satan's seat is" (Rev. 2:13). Apollonius traveled Asia Minor, healing and preaching, like Jesus traveled Palestine. The "seat" of paganism in Asia Minor was in Pergamos. There was a huge "altar of Zeus" and other various shrines. In *The Epistles of Apollonius*, Apollyon writes often to the elders of princes of Pergamos, thanking them for their hospitality, and admonishing them in various ways. In Pergamos the emperors erected temples in Apollyon's honour and worshipped him "as a god."[27]

Apollonius did travel widely outside Asia Minor (now modern Turkey). Philostratus records that when Apollonius came to the borders of Babylon, the king there refused to let him pass. Apollonius said to him: "All the earth is mine, and I have a right to go over it and through it." The king shrunk like a frightened child. This sounds mysteriously familiar. Remember what Lucifer was doing when the Lord asked, "Whence comest thou? Then Satan answered the Lord, and said, From going to and fro in the earth, and from walking up and down in it" (Job 1:7).

As already noted, Apollonius studied medicine and divining at the Temple of Aesculapius in Pergamos, Asia Minor. The Reverend Alexander Hislop; in his book *The Two Babylons*, discusses this temple and its meaning:[28]

> Now, the reader has seen already that another form of the sun divinity, or Teitan, at Rome, was worshipped under the name of others than himself, for that he was resolved never to wed nor have any connection whatever with women. In laying such a restraint on himself he surpassed Sophocles, who only said that in reaching old age he had escaped from a mad

and cruel master; but Apollonius by dint of
virtue and temperance never even in his youth
was so overcome.

Catholic priests and Hindu sages may work to suppress
and overcome their desire for women. Homosexuals pervert
that desire for women into an unnatural desire for men.
Apollonius, however, is the only one on record that we have
of a man who literally had no desire for women.

## HE SHALL CAUSE FIRE TO COME DOWN FROM HEAVEN

John writes of the Antichrist in his book of Revelation that
he will do miracles and "great wonders, so that he maketh fire
come down from heaven on the earth in the sight of men"
(Rev. 13:13). Jesus said to his disciples "I beheld Satan as
lightening fall from heaven" (Luke 10:18). We all know that
Satan is the great imitator. If God came down among men,
then Satan will as well. God incarnated himself as Jesus of
Nazareth. The sign of his birth was a star in the heavens.
Satan will not incarnate, but he will possess. Could it be that
he entered and possessed the body of Apollonius of Tyana?

Jesus tells us that lightening falling to earth is a sign of
Satan. In that context, read what Richard Cavendish, a scholar
on Hinduism, says. "In the *Mahabharata* the god Vishnu
reveals himself in a flash of lightening as bright as the light of
a thousand suns, and we are told that 'by penetrating this light
mortals skilled in yoga attain final deliverance'."[29] And again
Flavius Philostratus asserts:

> Now he is said to have been born in a meadow,
> hard by which has been now erected a
> sumptuous temple to him; and let us not pass
> by the manner of his birth.... the people of the
> country say that just at the moment of birth, a
> thunderbolt seemed about to fall to earth and
> then rose up into the air and disappeared aloft;
> and the gods thereby indicated, I think, the
> great distinction to which the sage was to

attain, and hinted in advance how he should
transcend all things upon earth and approach
the gods.... The people of the country,
then, say that Apollonius was a son of
this Zeus....[30]

Another translator renders the same words as, "the
moment of her delivery a lightening flash was seen to strike
the earth. . . ."[31] Does this indicate Satan falling to earth to
possess the man? We know that Apollonius performed many
satanic miracles. Eusebius, the ancient Christian historian,
writes that Apollonius performed "miracles due to the
cooperation of evil demons."[32]

## HE SHALL BE WORSHIPPED AS GOD

We have already seen that many people worshipped
Apollonius as a god. Apollonius crowned Vespasian, and told
him that "you need a man to administer and care for the
universe of such souls, a god sent down by wisdom."[33]
Philostratus tells of his birth:

While his mother was pregnant with him she
had a vision of Proteus, the Egyptian god who
turns himself into various shapes, according to
Homer. Unterrified by the apparition she asked
it what her child would be, and he replied
"myself." On her asking "Who are you?" he
answered: "the Egyptian god, Proteus." I need
not describe the wisdom of Proteus to those
who know from the poets how subtle he was,
and how many sided and elusive, and how he
seemed to know and to foreknow
everything.[34]

Do not forget that Moses called the serpent "more subtle
than any beast" in the field (Gen. 3:1). Proteus could change
shape at will. What was his favorite shape? Need you ask? It
was the serpent! Eusebius says that Apollonius could "read
the thoughts of men" and was "like their god Apollo."
Philostratus says that Apollonius "lived in the temples" that

he visited. He even received a letter from Caesar that said: "You may visit all the temples, and written instructions shall be sent by me to the priests who minister in them to admit you and adopt your reforms."[35] Did he visit the Temple of God in Jerusalem? That shall be covered in volume three of The Last Days Trilogy: *Apocalypse Unsealed.*

## THE NUMBER OF HIS NAME SHALL BE 666

Probably no other verse has mystified, aggravated, awed, or astounded students and scholars of the Bible than Revelation 13:18:

> Here is wisdom. Let him that hath under-
> standing count the number of the beast: for it
> is the number of a man: and his number is Six
> hundred threescore and six.

Since John wrote it, Christians have applied this to everyone from Nero to a computer in Belgium. The latest "candidates" for the "666" name are both Ronald Reagan and Mikhail Gorbachev (Henry Kissinger also "qualified" a few years back). However, we must ask ourselves: "What did John mean by it?" If John was speaking of a man who was to come thousands of year in the future, then why did he admonish his readers to figure out the name themselves? Could it be that John was writing of a man the Christians (in Asia Minor) would easily recognize.

The Arabs introduced the symbols we now call numbers in the late Middle Ages. Before that, people used letters for numbers. For example: The Hebrew letter *Aleph* represented the number one, and the same is true for the Greek letter *a.* Somehow, the number of the beast and the number of the man will both be 666.

What did John mean? Did he mean a man whose numerical number of his name equals 666? If that were true, then perhaps fifty million people alive today would "qualify." Did he mean a computer or a system that would appear far in the future? If that's true, his words are ambiguous, for he told Christians living then to "count the number of the beast." How could they do that if the "beast" wasn't to come around for hundreds or thousands of years afterward? It is believed by some that the beast, as well as the man, were well-known to John and the Christians living in Asia Minor (It is to the seven churches in Asia Minor that the book of Revelation is addressed.)

What is the beast? Reverend Hislop may have some clues. He declares that it applies to Saturn. He writes:

> As Mystery signifies the Hidden system, so Saturn signifies the Hidden god. To those who were initiated the god was revealed; to all else he was hidden. Now, the name Saturn in Chaldee is pronounced Satur; but, as every Chaldee scholar knows, consists only of four letters, thus—S T U R—This name contains exactly the Apocalyptic number: 666.
>
> | S | = | 60 |
> | T | = | 400 |
> | U | = | 6 |
> | R | = | 200 |
>
> The name "Lat," or the hidden one, had evidently been given, as well as Saturn, to the Great Babylonian god.... the sun-god Apollo had been known under the name of Lat...The Indian god Siva... is sometimes represented as... the Roman Saturn....[36]

In Hinduism, Siva (pronounced Shee-vah) is the *Destroyer* aspect of the Trinity. Lateinos also adds to 666. But this still doesn't answer the question. Hislop writes that "it was long ago noticed by Irenaeus, about the end of the second century, that the name Teitan contained the Mystic number 666; and he gave it as his opinion that Teitan was "by far the most probable name of the beast from the sea."[37]

Irenaeus was a Christian who learned Christianity at the feet of Polycarp who, in turn, learned the faith at the feet of John the Revelator. Hislop goes on to say that "the Chaldean

[Babylonian] Mysteries came westward to Asia Minor. . . . Teitan was just a synonym for Typhon, the malignant Serpent or Dragon. . . ." Hislop finally writes, "Now, the reader has seen already that another form of the sun divinity, or Teitan, at Rome, was the Epidaurian snake, worshipped under the name of 'Aeculapius', that is, the man instructing serpent."[38]

Pagans believe that Apollonius was the incarnation of Aesculapius. The name Teitan also equals 666 in the Greek. The name Apollo-Python represented the sun-god, Saturn, in his two forms—one light and one dark. Apollo represented the light of the day—goodness, health, dryness, life. Python represented the god at night—darkness, evil, wetness, and death. Apollo-Python was the Lord of Death. Whether beast (Teitan) or man, the number of the name equaled 666. Christians and pagans living in Asia Minor could have recognized this without a great deal of trouble.

## APOLLONIUS-THE PAGAN CHRIST?

Next I checked scholars and historians, Christian and non-Christian, to see what they had to say about Apollonius. What they had to say only confirmed my suspicions. Here are a few examples:

*Prof. J. M. Robertson:*

>	Apollonius lived in the first century of our era. By the third century a wealth of legend surrounded his name. He was believed to have had a supernatural birth, to have worked many miracles, to have made converts in Europe and Asia, and finally to have ascended to heaven. He has been plausibly described as a "Pagan Christ."[39]

*Prof. G. R. S. Mead:*

>	There may have been only a few years between the birth of Jesus and of Apollonius, and the curious parallels between their lives have caused much religious controversy, some believing that incidents in the life of Apollonius were myths thrown up by Christianity, others suggesting that the

Christians had borrowed earlier stories concerning
Apollonius for their Gospels. For centuries,
religious argument raged around the figure of
Apollonius. Was he divine or charlatan, saint or
magician? Was he better or worse than Jesus of
Nazareth? Apollonius was regarded as a serious
religious rival to Jesus Christ, and even as late as
seventeenth century, there were freethinkers like
Voltaire who extolled his teachings above those of
Christianity. [40]

*Dr. F. W. Groves Campbell:*

Both Apollonius of Tyana and Jesus of
Nazareth were born in the same year; both Tyana's
babe and the Bethlehem's were said to have sprung
from a divine Father and a human mother; and both
these holy ones drew their first breaths amid
gracious portents and supernatural singing. Nor
were these the only parallels in the memoirs of the
Tyanean and the Nazarene. [41]

Mead says that since the forth century the character of
Apollonius was regarded with little favor, and that "many have
been taught to look upon our philosopher not only as a
charlatan, but even as an Antichrist." [42] F. C. Conybeare wrote
in another work of his, *The Origins of Christianity*, that while
Jesus was casting out demons in Palestine "Apollonius of
Tyana was casting out demons in Syria . . . These demons
talked just as they do in Mark's narrative, and the stories of
Apollonius, which are probably from the pen of his
Syro-Greek disciple Damis, read like pages of our Mark or
Matthew." [43] Here are a few other scholars commenting:

*Dr. Gerhard Uhlhorn:*

A heathen Church organized itself in
opposition to the Christian Church, and, to push the
parallel to the utmost, there was put forward a
heathen Christ.... Apollonius of Tyana, for we find
him exhibited as a veritable heathen Christ. The

historical Apollonius was a magician and necromancer, who spent his life journeying about and plying his magic arts... In the reign of Septimius Severus, Flavius Philostratus wrote a biography of this Apollonius, in which, by the most fanciful idealization, he is set forth as a counterpart and rival of Christ. His mother bore him to the god Proteus.... He acquired the wisdom of India in that land, and then began his progress through the world in order to reform Heathenism. He drew disciples around him, preached in the principal cities of the Roman Empire, and performed numerous miracles....

The miracles which Philostratus relates are often very similar to Christ's miracles. In Rome, for instance, Apollonius met a funeral procession; a young girl lay upon the bier; her bridegroom followed weeping, accompanied by many friends. Apollonius stopped the procession, asked the name of the dead, then touched the corpse, and spoke a few words. Immediately the young girl arose, as if she had awaked from sleep. His preaching inculcated the reform of Heathenism....

There can be no doubt that we have here a representation drawn with the full intention of constructing a heathen counterpart of Christ. Philostratus was not, like Lucian, merely writing a satire, but he was seriously making the attempt to set up a heathen Christ in opposition to the Christian Christ.[44]

## APOLLONIUS VS. JESUS

Apollonius was clearly put forth as the "counterpart" of the Christian Christ. He was the heathen, or pagan Christ. Since pagans worship Lucifer, they can properly be called

Luciferians. Apollonius was the Luciferian "Christ." Since Satan is the great imitator, the pagan Christ was to imitate the true Christ.

Jesus taught that he fulfilled the Law and the Prophets. He taught us to obey him, and to love one another. Apollonius taught necromancy, astrology, reincarnation, healing with crystals, and "Social Darwinism." Apollonius crowned Roman emperors who then deified themselves, and sent misery to multitudes. Jesus fed multitudes of the poor, and gave them streams of living waters. Apollonius praised the Brahmin (God-men) of India those who lived lives of luxury by enslaving the lower castes. Jesus ate with publicans and sinners, and called all men to worship together as brothers. Apollonius called the "Self" god. Jesus said that he who worships self shall die, but he that loses his self in service to others shall live (Luke 18:14). As you read these next chapters, the significance of what I have written in this chapter, will become apparent.

## *SECOND ADVENTS*

Today, Christians await the second advent of Jesus of Nazareth. We know that he will come in the clouds with great power and glory. On the opposite side, Luciferians (occultists) expect the return of Apollonius. They call him Kalki, The Destroyer. I believe a rational argument can be advanced that Maitreya is this destroyer.

What is Maitreya saying? In one of Maitreya's channeled messages to Benjamin Creme, he says, "Manifest around you That which I pronounce and become as Gods." Compare this to the proclamation of the serpent [Satan] to Eve in the Garden of Eden:

> And the serpent said unto the woman, Ye shall not surely die: For God doth know that in the day ye eat thereof, then your eyes shall be opened, and ye shall be as gods. (Gen. 3:4-5)

If Satan possessed the man Apollonius two thousand years ago, then he will possess another in these last days. Is he now here? What is in store for the earth in the next few years? I will try to answer these questions in the rest of this book. I will also identify the man whom Benjamin Creme knows as Maitreya, the New Age "Messiah," in part 6.

# 2.

# PART TWO

## What Do We Know About Lord Maitreya?

The ads which boldly proclaimed "THE CHRIST IS NOW HERE" went on to say that "the Christ" would make his identity known to the world "within two months." The hoped for "Day of Declaration" did not arrive as scheduled. This reminds us of Moses' admonition in the Bible: "When a prophet speaketh in the name of the LORD, if the thing follow not, nor come to pass, that is the thing which the LORD hath not spoken, but the prophet hath spoken it presumptuously; thou shalt not be afraid of him" (Deut. 18:22).

Maitreya (pronounced "My-tray-uh") specified a time and place in which he would present himself to the world. Over sixty journalists from a dozen countries appeared in London to interview him. But Maitreya never appeared. Creme blamed the "no show" on insufficient media attention. I know the real reason (I will explain in detail later) the event was cancelled. Many Christians have taken the attitude that either the danger is over, or that the entire affair was some sort of elaborate joke. I am here to tell you that it was no joke! After the first event failed, it's organizers grew more determined that "next time" the entire world would take notice. For those unfamiliar with the remarkable events of April 1982, let me explain. The ad said, in so many words:

- The world needs help to solve global problems.
- The "Christ" is now here to offer the only solutions.
- This "Christ" is called Maitreya.
- He is the "Promised One" of all religions, and of no religion.
- Only a few disciples, called the "Masters of Wisdom," know who he is.
- He shall soon identify himself via international radio and television broadcast, which everyone will hear in his own language.

An organization called the Tara Center placed the ads. Creme admitted that the ads cost over a quarter of a million dollars. From Tokyo to Tucson, and from Karachi to California, millions of people gasped over the startling "news" when they opened their morning papers.

## *FROM NEW AGE TO ROCK OF AGE*

I was raised a Theosophist (the premier Aquarian missionary society). I was taught to view Christians, or at least the"fundamentalist" variety, as bizarre, fanatical, ignorant, and, above all, dangerous. My schooling, in the California public school system, only confirmed the attitude taught to me at home. It wasn't until I had become friends with some Fundamentalists, that I began to doubt some of the things taught to me about Christianity. In my young adulthood I became an ardent student of the occult. I initiated several of my friends into the occult. Later, after I became a born-again believer, I used the contacts and knowledge that I had in the occult to go "undercover" back into the New Age. Why? Because I needed to discover the identity of Maitreya, and what sort of plans New Agers were making for the world in which I am a part.

As an Aquarian, I worked for the Tara Center at their base
in Los Angeles, California.  Naturally, I was upset when
"Maitreya" didn't show in June of 1982, but I didn't show it.
I kept on working and making excuses with the others.  We
blamed his "no show" on everything from "bad Karmic
vibrations" to accusing the media of not taking us seriously,
and that is why. . . . etc.  Then I heard from others there about
a "fundamentalist fanatic" by the name of Constance Cumbey.
We made jokes about her.  One day someone brought to me
a copy of her book: *The Hidden Dangers of the Rainbow.*  I
laughed at it, but later I became curious.  Within three days I
had read it twice from cover to cover.  Soon afterward I was
out of the Tara Center, and on my way to becoming one of
those "fanatical" fundamentalist Christians.

## WHO IS BENJAMIN CREME?

The Tara Center is the "press office" for one man:
Benjamin Creme, the "latter-day John the Baptist."  He sees
himself as the forerunner of Maitreya (the New Age
"Messiah").  Here is what the January 1982 issue of
*Emergence*, the official newsletter of the Tara Center, has to
say about him: "Benjamin Creme is a 58 year old Scot, an
artist by profession.  Since his early youth, he has been
interested in the esoteric, the area of the ageless wisdom that
has been transmitted from one generation to the next.  In 1959,
he received a telepathic message from his Master, a member
of the hierarchy—an event that came as a complete surprise
to him . . . Later, Creme received communications that came
directly from Maitreya himself.  In 1975, he was given the
mission of announcing publicly the coming of Maitreya. . . ."

In an attempt to "increase the energy" that comes from
Maitreya and other Masters, the Tara Centers have established
something that they call "transmission groups"—meetings in
which group meditation is focused as an aid in passing on the
energies of the "Hierarchy"(spiritually perfected beings who
rule the world) to large numbers of people, thus preparing the
spiritual climate for the reappearance of "the Christ."  The idea

of transmission groups receiving energy through positive mental images into the mainstream of human consciousness is obviously occult in nature. There is definitely spiritual power involved. And if, in fact, spiritual energies are being transmitted through the estimated hundreds, perhaps thousands of people involved in these transmission groups around the world, there must be some purpose to it.

The Tara Centers are centers for the dissemination of information about Maitreya, the alleged "Christ," as well as bases of operation for Benjamin Creme, and headquarters for the establishment of transmission groups. They are also engaged in seeking to alleviate the problem of world hunger by promoting the idea of sharing, involving themselves closely with Share International. Share International works in cooperation with The Hunger Project, based in San Francisco, and founded in 1977 by Werner Erhard, founder of EST. (Contrary to what many may think, The Hunger Project is not just a charitable organization that feeds the poor. It is an organization that works to influence people's thinking toward redistribution of wealth.)

The concern of these people for the poor, of course, is admirable. We do not criticize them for this. However, Creme's teachings regarding the natures of God and man, the person of Jesus Christ, salvation, incarnation and spiritual matters on the whole are contrary to biblical theology and must be challenged. It's tragic, but the good works of Benjamin Creme and his associates are lending undeserved credibility to their false teachings.

## WHO IS LORD MAITREYA?

For anyone unfamiliar with the esoteric (the occult), the name "Maitreya" may seem very foreign. The Tara Center states that "the Buddha with a waterpot demonstrates the concepts, 'Maitreya' by which name the Buddhists expect an avatar, and 'aquarian', have been related to one another since antiquity." In other words, to occultists there have been nine avatars, or incarnations of the godhead. Westerners have probably heard of Krishna, the 8th avatar, and Buddha, the 9th. Orientals await Maitreya, who shall be the 10th and final avatar.The word "Maitreya is from the sacred language of the Hindus, Sanskrit, and it means "Merciful One." Yet, as we shall see, he shall be anything but merciful.

According to Creme, Maitreya is "the Christ, Head of our planetary Hierarchy."[1] Christians might better think of him as "the god of this world" (2 Cor. 4:4). Creme calls Jesus, Maitreya's chief disciple: "The Disciple Jesus, Who is now the Master Jesus, was born in Palestine as a third degree initiate. . . .[2] He was, and still is, a Disciple of the Christ and made the great sacrifice of giving up His body for use by the Christ. By the occult process of overshadowing, the Christ, Maitreya, took over the body of Jesus from baptism onward."[3]

In other words, Jesus is not the Christ, but a "disciple" of the Christ! According to Creme, Jesus gave up his body to be "possessed"by "the Christ." The Bible asks, "Who is a liar but he that denieth that Jesus is the Christ? He is Antichrist, that denieth the Father and the Son" (1 John 2:22). Creme continues:

> The normal method, or the most frequent, for the manifestation of an avatar, is to take over the body of a disciple, as happened with Jesus. The Christ, Maitreya, remained in the Himalayas, but His consciousness, or some aspect of His consciousness, whatever was needed at the time, took over the body of the Disciple Jesus and worked through Him for the last three years of His life. This time He has come as Himself.[4] In the esoteric tradition, the Christ is not the name of an individual but an Office in the Hierarchy. The present holder of that Office, the Lord Maitreya, has held it for 2,600 years, and manifested in Palestine through His Disciple, Jesus, by the occult method of Overshadowing, the most frequent form used for the manifestation of Avatars. He

has never left the world, but for 2,000 years
has waited and planned for this time, training
His Disciples and preparing Himself for the
awesome task that awaits Him. He has made
it known that this time, He himself will come.[5]

We see immediately what this esoteric view of the Christ
does to the biblical Jesus. It seeks to strip him of his divinity
as the Word of God incarnate (John 1:1-4), the Christ sent to
redeem men from their sins. Creme makes a frontal assault
against the Gospel and the true Jesus:

People have been led to leave the Churches in
large numbers because the Churches have
presented a picture of the Christ impossible for
most thinking people today to accept—as the
One and Only Son of God, sacrificed by His
loving Father to save Humanity from the
results of its sins; as a Blood Sacrifice straight
out of the old and outworn Jewish Dispensa-
tion; as the unique revealer of God's nature,
once and forever, never to be enlarged and
expanded as man himself grows in awareness
and ability to receive other revelations of that
Divine nature; and as waiting in some mythical
and unattractive Heaven until the end of the
world, when He will return in a cloud of glory
to the sound of Angel's trumpets, and, des-
cending from these clouds, inherit His
Kingdom. The majority of thinking people
today have rejected this view... The view put
forth by esotericism is surely more rational and
acceptable and more in line with modern
man's knowledge of history and science and
of religions other than Christianity.[6] He
[Jesus] is not the one and only Son of God, but
the friend and Elder Brother of Humanity.[7]

The conflict is in reality then, Christianity standing alone
against the philosophies of the world. Such philosophies reject

the infallibility of the Bible in its revelation of God, of Jesus as the begotten Son of God, of the nature and destiny of man and his relationship to God as Creator, apart from creation.

## HOW WILL MAITREYA COME?

Benjamin Creme's writings are replete with information on how Maitreya will manifest himself:

> He came into the world by aeroplane and so fulfilled prophesy of "coming in the clouds." On July 8th 1977, He descended from the Himalayas into the Indian sub-continent and went to one of the chief cities. He had an acclimatization period between July 8th and 18th, and then, on the 19th, entered a certain modern country by aeroplane. He is now an ordinary man in the world—an extraordinary, ordinary man.[8]

## WHO IS THE REAL CHRIST?

Let's consider what the Bible says, keeping in mind that it is the written Word of God. It is also an extraordinary compilation of sixty-six books, written over a period of some eighteen hundred years by various authors, yet all the while proving itself historically and prophetically flawless—in perfect harmony in all its teachings from beginning to end.

The skeptic will argue that the Bible has undergone numerous translations and rewriting, and thus is not credible. But if God can give his Word, he can keep it intact and, in fact, has done so. His Holy Spirit gives understanding to any who read it with an honest heart, seeking after truth (Heb. 11:6). The proof of the integrity of Scripture is one hundred percent accuracy in its prophecies of future events. The only Scripture unfulfilled are those that pertain to the Lord's return and the events that will occur thereafter. It is foolish, therefore, to ignore or reject the words of the Bible, words that reveal to us who God truly is, and what our relationship to him should be.

Creme expressed his opinion of the Bible at a press conference held at the Ambassador Hotel in Los Angeles, on May 14, 1982. In response to a reporter's question about whether his views of Christ and the Bible might be considered Antichrist, or anti-Bible, Creme commented that the Bible is a great book of truth. However, he feels that, taken literally, it is nonsensical. It can only be understood by one possessing esoteric knowledge obtained through initiation into the mystery religions. He also reiterated his belief that Jesus is not the Christ. But God's Word says, "Who is a liar but he that denies that Jesus is the Christ?" (1John 2:22).

Creme also claims that "the Christ" is a Senior Member of the hierarchy, a Master of Wisdom. Yet God's Word, proven infallible, declares:

> For God so loved the world that he gave his only begotten Son, that whosoever believes in him should not perish, but have everlasting life (John 3:16). In the beginning was the Word, and the Word was with God, and the Word was God...All things were made by him; and without him was not any thing made that was made....And the Word was made flesh, and dwelt among us....(John 1:1,3,14)

When the wise men from the east came to Herod seeking "he that is born King of the Jews," Herod inquired of the chief priests and scribes where the Christ (not one of his disciples!) was to be born, as Matthew reports: "And they said unto him, In Bethlehem of Judea; for thus it is written by the prophet [Micah] (Matt. 2:1-6).

Jesus, therefore, is the Christ, the Word of God, who did come into the world to redeem men from sin and its consequences, contrary to Creme's assertion. There are over 550 references to the Christ in the New Testament alone. All refer to the person of Jesus of Nazareth. When Peter acknowledged him as "the Christ, the Son of the Living God" in Matthew 16:16, Jesus did not say, "I am not the Christ, but only the disciple of Maitreya." He said, "Blessed art thou Simon Barjona: for flesh and blood hath not revealed it unto thee, but my Father which is in heaven" (Matt. 16:17).

While Creme claims that "the Christ," Maitreya, is the same as the Jew's Messiah, the Hindus' Krishna, the Buddhists' 'fifth Buddha," the Moslems' "Imam Mahdi, and the Christians' Christ, God's Word says that "there is no other name under heaven given to men by which we must be saved" (Acts 4:10-12).

> Wherefore God also hath highly exalted him, and given him a name which is above every other name: That at the name of Jesus every knee should bow, of things in heaven, and things in earth, and things under the earth; And that every tongue should confess that Jesus Christ is Lord, to the glory of God the Father. (Phil. 2:9-11)

The name of Jesus is exalted above every name, including the name Maitreya. Jesus Christ is Lord, not Maitreya. These Scriptures were written under the inspiration of the Holy Spirit some thirty years after Jesus' ministry on earth. Creme's allegations that Jesus was the Christ for only three years is, therefore, erroneous.

## HOW WILL THE REAL CHRIST COME?

Now let's compare the coming of Creme's "Christ" to the Bible's account of how the true Christ, Jesus, will come again. The prophetical events that shall precede his return are of importance:

> Immediately after the tribulation of those days shall the sun be darkened and the moon shall not give her light, and the stars shall fall from heaven, and the powers of the heavens shall be shaken: And then shall appear the sign of the Son of man in heaven, and then shall all the tribes of the earth mourn, and they shall see the Son of man coming in the clouds of heaven

with power and great glory. And he shall send
his angels with a great sound of a trumpet, and
they shall gather together his elect from the
four winds, from one end of heaven to the
other. (Matt.24: 29-31) (Also see Mark 13:
19 & Rev. 6:12-17)

The Apostle Paul tells us what will become of God's
people when Jesus returns, "Behold, I shew you a mystery;
We shall not all sleep (die) but we shall all be changed, in a
moment, in the twinkling of an eye, at the last trump: for the
trumpet shall sound, and the dead shall be raised incorruptible,
and we shall be changed" (1 Cor. 15:51-52).

The scriptural accounts of the Lord's return hardly sound
like some secret arrival by airplane. They reveal, rather, that
the nations will see him come in the clouds and will mourn
because they know his judgment is coming with him. And
rather than suggesting that God's people must go through a
gradual evolutionary change through reincarnation, the Bible
is clear in its teaching that the dead will be resurrected and
those living at the time of Christ's return will be changed
immediately "in the twinkling of an eye." The author of the
book of Hebrews refutes the concept of reincarnation. "And
as it is appointed unto men once to die, but after this the
judgment: So Christ was once offered to bear the sins of many;
and unto them that look for him shall he appear the second
time without [bearing] sin unto salvation" (Heb. 9:27-28).

Concerning the resurrection, even the esotericists have
their ideas, of which Christians should be aware. Speaking of
the Shroud of Turin, Creme says he believes "it is . . .
authentic . . ." Creme's words might mislead some.

> It is the shroud in which the body of Jesus was
> wrapped after the crucifixion. The image on it
> was deposited intentionally and left there for
> future generations to hold to the reality of
> resurrection, because that is what the whole

gospel story is about. The gospel story is not about crucifixion. It is about resurrection.[9]

Actually, the Gospel story is about both—the crucifixion and the resurrection. Even so, these words of Creme might confuse some into thinking he has a proper concept of the importance of the resurrection—until we read further: "Resurrection will be the emphasized goal for mankind; resurrection out of matter into Spirit, which makes one a liberated Master."[10] In his press conference at the Ambassador Hotel, Creme further reinforced his lack of belief in a physical resurrection. He ridiculed the idea with the allegation that no particular body could possibly be resurrected since man is reincarnated into different bodies repeatedly.

Here we see a genuine delineation between the truth of the Gospel and the lies of the cults. True Christians believe in the resurrection of the body. Jehovah's Witnesses, Moonies, all the various cults and aberrations of Christian thought, deny the reality of the physical resurrection. Some Mormons claim to believe in the resurrection of the body, but their error lines up with the esotericists in their belief that God is a man who advanced to a higher level of perfection. Not dissimilar to Creme's and other secret temple teachings of the esoteric mystery religions. Only those who hold to the Scriptures as God's revelation, have any chance of not being deceived.

## THE HIERARCHY

In previous quotes from Creme's writings he mentions "the Hierarchy." According to Creme, there is a spiritual "Hierarchy" comprised of "the Masters, the Initiates and the disciples of the world."[11]

These "Masters" are "The Masters of Wisdom," men who, through thousands of years of evolutionary progress and many incarnations, have advanced to a high degree of stewardship over the cosmos. Creme says that "there is a Hierarchy throughout the system, in fact throughout the cosmos. Our Hierarchy was brought into this planet by the Lord of the World, about seventeen million years ago, to oversee the development of early man, individualized about one million years later."[12]

Creme speaks of "the Lord of the World" whose dwelling place is "Shamballa"—"the *will* aspect of Deity." Could this "Lord of this World" be the same Lord we Christians worship as the true Christ, the Word of God, sent from the Father to atone for our sins?

Jesus said, "My kingdom is not of this world" (John 18:36). Satan, the deceiver and instigator of rebellion against God, is called "the god of this world," and "the prince of this world." As the writer of Corinthians suggests:

> In whom the god of this world hath blinded the minds of them which believe not, lest the light of the glorious gospel of Christ, who is the image of God, should shine unto them. (2 Cor. 4:4)

And again:

> Now is the judgment of this world: now shall the prince of this world be cast out. (John 12:31)

Benjamin Creme speaks of an ever changing "Hierarchy" working within the framework of deity; But God says, "I am the Lord, *I change not*" (Mal. 3:6). Benjamin Creme also speaks of "Initiation" into the Mystery Religion of his "Lord Maitreya." God says: "I have not spoken in secret, in a dark place of the earth . . . I the Lord speak righteousness I declare things that are right" (Isa. 45:19).

The way of salvation is open to all men. It is not necessary for them to go through initiation and constant search. The things of God that are hidden must remain hidden, for the infinite cannot be searched out by finite minds. Thus the Lord also says, "The secret things belong unto the Lord" (Deut. 29:29).

The principalities and powers against whom Paul says we wrestle (Eph. 6:12), are the same spiritual forces that have guided mankind's institutions—religious, scientific, economic, social, and governmental—throughout history. They have long had their adherents, people who choose to worship them instead of the one, true God. At their head is Lucifer, called Satan—the Destroyer—a spirit being who is the "prince of this world"—whose desire it was, because of pride, to be like the Most High God:

> How art thou fallen from heaven, O Lucifer, son of the morning. How art thou cut down to the ground, which didst weaken the nations.
>
> For thou hast said in thine heart, I will ascend into heaven, I will exalt my throne above the stars of God: I will sit also upon the mount of the congregation, in the sides of the north: I will ascend above the heights of the clouds; I will be like the most High. Yet thou shalt be brought down to hell, to the sides of the pit. (Isa. 14:12-15)

Lucifer's lies from the beginning have pervaded this world—part of his dominion within the cosmos from eons past. His attempt to remain in control of this planetary system has been the basis of the struggle between God and God's enemies ever since Lucifer's fall.

Lucifer—called Satan after the fall—tempted man with the lie that if he would pursue the knowledge of good and evil, he would be like God (Gen. 3:15). Man succumbed and thus entered onto the scene of human drama, the sin of man's rebellion—and the need for redemption.

Since that time, the struggle for men's souls has escalated and "the Lord of this World" has never put aside his original lie, "Follow me, and I will give you knowledge; I will make you a god."

This lie has, throughout history, marked the difference between the vast numbers of egocentric humans who have pursued the world's religions, and God's people who see their need for submission to God. Inversely, the Christian, Creme says, is the only one not compatible with the universal religion.

## THE GREAT TEMPTATION

> And the serpent (Satan) said unto the woman, Ye shall not surely die: For God doth know that in the day ye eat thereof, then your eyes shall be opened, and ye shall be as gods, knowing good and evil. (Gen. 3:4-5)

What is the central message Benjamin Creme claims to have received from "Lord Maitreya"? In a volume entitled *Messages from Maitreya the Christ*, Creme has transcribed recorded messages uttered during the many occasions Maitreya "overshadowed" him. Here are some excerpts:

> My friends, My children, I am here to show you that there exists for Man a most marvelous future. Decked in all the colours of the rainbow, glowing with the light of God, Man, one day, will stand upright in His Divinity....May this manifestation lead you to seek and to know that Self which is God.[13] Manifest around you That which I pronounce and become as Gods.

God's Word says, "I am God, and not man—the Holy One among you" (Hos. 11:9).

God is not a man; man is not God. Man is a creation of God, made from the elements of the earth to live on earth, not some ethereal plane. God's Word promises that when Jesus returns he will establish his government on earth for one thousand years to show man how to live righteously. After that time, all rebellion against God and his only Christ will be put down forever, God will create a new heaven and a new earth and we, his people, in resurrected bodies, will dwell on the earth for eternity with God in our midst (Rev. 21:22).

Adherents to the world's religions have no hope. If they are to be continually reincarnated to live their lives repeatedly until they get it right, forget it. No one has ever gotten it right except Jesus—the One who is God become man.

The pride of Lucifer and his angels to rebel against God is the same as the pride of man that seeks ways to perfection other than the one way provided by God—surrender to Jesus Christ and to the working of the Holy Spirit. God wants us to be exalted in the righteousness of Christ alone.

As perfect as the adepts of the world religion think they have become, they are fools if they don't realize that as they draw closer to Self, they draw farther from God. This, then, prompts them to believe they are suited to rule in the New Age as humanity's overseers.

## THE ROOTS OF DECEPTION

The metaphysical teachings of Benjamin Creme go back much further in time than might be thought. We have traced them to the mystery religions of Egypt and Babylon. Creme readily admits that the "Sphinx . . . and Pyramid . . . were connected with the Mysteries of Initiation." He even discusses Atlantean civilization.

> The Mystery Schools go back to Atlantean times. The process of Initiation was instituted in midAtlantean times, and the remains in Egypt, South America-Mexico, Peru, Caldea and Babylon, relate to these ancient civilizations. They are degenerated forms of it, for the Atlantean civilization was a tremendous, scientific civilization, such as the world has not seen since. In Egypt, the requirements of Initiation were known, but secretly there was no outer teaching as there is today. The ancient religion of Atlantis was what today we call spiritualism....The religion of ancient Egypt was, Spiritualism; the religion of China, for the last 4,000 years is a kind of Spiritualism.[14]

To show the connection between the ancient Mystery Religion and Creme's "Lord Maitreya" we need only quote Creme further:

> When the physical structures of human living are reconstructed and the principles that should govern our life in Aquarius are understood and being implemented, the Christ will reveal to man an entirely new aspect of Reality, a New Revelation, which it is His mission to bring. *The Ancient Mysteries will be restored, the Mystery Schools reopened, and a great expansion of man's awareness of himself and his purpose and destiny will become possible.*[15] [emphasis added]

> The Mystery schools will be reopened and men will go to them as they now go to University, to learn and to take the disciplines that will prepare them for initiation, and so into the Hierarchy.[16] The new religion will manifest itself through organizations like Masonry.

> Those systems can change in response to the pressures of the energies and ideas and ideals of the time will have a place. Eventually a new world religion will be inaugurated, which will be a fusion and synthesis of the approach of the East and the approach of the West. The Christ will bring together, not simply Christianity and Buddhism, but the concept of God transcendent—outside of His creation in man and all creation.

> It will be seen to be possible to hold both approaches at the same time, and they will be brought together in a new scientific religion based on the Mysteries; on Initiation; on Invocation....[17]

> Gradually, Christianity, Buddhism and other religions will wither away-slowly, as the people die out of them, as the new religion gains its adherents and exponents, and is gradually built by humanity.[18]

So says Benjamin Creme. Yet the Bible tells us in many places that the Mystery religions of Egypt and Babylon are an abomination to God, and they will one day be destroyed:

> When you come into the land which the Lord your God gives you, you shall not learn to do after the abominations of those nations. There shall not be found among you anyone that makes his son or his daughter pass through the fire, or that uses divination, or an observer of times, or an enchanter, or a witch, or a charmer, or a consulter with familiar spirits, or a wizard, or a necromancer. For all that do these things are an abomination to the Lord; and because of these abominations the Lord your God drives them out before you (Deut. 18:9-12). He shall break also the images of Beth-shemesh, that is in the land of Egypt; and the houses of the gods of the Egyptians shall he burn with fire (Jer. 43:13).

> You provoke me unto wrath with the works of your hands, burning incense unto other gods in the land of Egypt. (Jer. 44:8)

> Against all the gods of Egypt I will execute judgment: I am the Lord. (Exodus 12:12)

As for the Lord's prophecies concerning the fate of Creme's religious system, a system gleaned from Egypt and Babylon, John the Revelator tells us it is doomed (See Rev. 17:1). Creme and millions of occult members are promoting a religious system predicted by God, which will flaunt its humanistic philosophy and make war against God's people on earth, the Church.

Creme, himself, gives a clue to this future holocaust when he says, "The view put forth by esotericism is surely more rational and acceptable and more in line with modern man's knowledge of history and service and of religions other than Christianity"[19] And, coupled with his remark that "Gradually, Christianity, Buddhism and other religions will wither away-slowly as people die out of them . . ." We see the very real possibility of aquarianity taking steps to speed up its takeover by persecution and execution of those who resist its advancement.

## *THE CREME CHRONOLOGY*

Here is a summary of what Creme has been preaching, and what Maitreya has been predicting since this all started back in 1982. This will bring the reader up-to-date on the events surrounding the New Age movement and their bid to install Maitreya as "Lord" of the world. In summary, Creme is saying:

1) All the great religions look forward to a future World Teacher. The Jews await the Messiah, the Muslims the Imam Mahdi, the Christians await the return of Jesus, and the Hindus await Krishna in his incarnation as Kalki. The Buddhists await Maitreya. The name itself means "Merciful One." Jesus was the World Teacher for the Piscean Age. We are now entering the Aquarian Age, and, thus, a new World Teacher should be expected.

2) The Hierarchy gave the first information about the World Teacher to the Masters of Wisdom, who channeled this information to H.P. Blavatsky, and later Alice Bailey of the Theosophical Society.

3) Maitreya once possessed the body of Jesus. Now Maitreya possesses the body of a man from Pakistan. He travelled by plane from Karachi, Pakistan, to London,

England.  He is a member of the Pakistani community in London at this time.

4) Benjamin Creme presented information about Maitreya's emergence to the public in 1974.

To summarize the historical perspective: May 14, 1982: Creme reveals during a press conference in Los Angeles that Maitreya lives in the Asian community in London and invites the media of the world to locate him.  1982-1985:  For short periods various freelance journalists make attempts to find Maitreya.  July 31, 1985: A corps of twenty-two journalists, representing a dozen countries, gather in London's east end to discuss the methods of making Maitreya's "Day of Declaration" possible.  1986:  Top executives of the British media agree to stage the "Day of Declaration," but are prevented by higher authorities in the British government.  1987:  Benjamin Creme announces that Maitreya, to prove his divinity, will give several prophecies to be published in *Share International* magazine.  1988:  Maitreya allegedly appears both in person and in dreams, to well known leaders in various countries, and among ordinary citizens.  June 11:  Maitreya appears in Nairobi, Kenya, and is photographed addressing thousands of people who kneel down to worship him.

Maitreya, through *Share International*, announces that within a matter of months all foreign troops shall withdraw from Angola.  (This occurred as predicted.)

June:  Maitreya announces that "a compromise" would be reached between Iran and Iraq, and that war would soon end. Within a few months the war ended.

November:  Maitreya declares that "There will be a major earthquake in the USSR."  On December 7 the Armenian quake struck.

Maitreya predicted that Nelson Mandela would soon be released. This occurred as predicted.

Maitreya has also made other predictions that have come to pass; he has also made some *false predictions*, such as:

1) Mikail Gorbachev would have an assassination attempted upon him, and be removed from office. The date came and went.

2) Anglican Church envoy, and hostage, Terry Waite would be released. This did not occur.

I could give you other examples, but, remember, the Bible says that a prophet is false even if he gives only "one" false prophecy (Deut. chapter 18).

## THE FORCE

As we have seen, according to the Bible, Maitreya cannot possibly be "the Christ" of God. The "God" of the occultists is not the God of the Bible. This is the "god" that the esotericists, like Creme, believe in:

> God always works through agents. Always.
> This is true for every manifestation of God. As
> soon as God comes into incarnation, manifests
> *itself* at whatever level, *it* works through some
> agency or other. *Itself it* manifests and yet it
> is immanent in everything that is manifest[20]
> (emphasis added).

Notice that Creme refers to his "god" as "It" instead of "He." Occultists believe that "God" is an impersonal "Force" that is both good and evil, light and dark. The Nazis, who were deep into the occult, also believed this. Martin Bormann, the head of the German Nazi Party Organization, declared:

> If we National Socialists (Nazis) speak about
> "faith in God" we do not mean the same God
> as the naive Christians....The natural Force
> which maintains these innumerable planets in
> the universe we call the Almighty God.[21]

In 1945, Dr. Robert Ley, head of the Nazi Labor Front, left a message for the future Germany just before committing suicide in his prison cell: "We have forsaken God, and therefore we were forsaken by God. We put our human volition in place of His Godly grace."[22] To Aquarians, "God" can be light or dark. To Christians, God is Light, and has *no* darkness at all. The Bible says: "This then is the message we have heard of him [Jesus] and declare unto you, that God is light, and in him is no darkness." Since Lucifer can change himself into an "angel of light" it should not surprise Christians that Aquarians see their "god" as both light and dark.

## IS MAITREYA THE ANTICHRIST?

Creme has written:

> The gradual expansion of Maitreya's activities will lead to a world press conference which will in turn lead to the Day of His Declaration. Then, He will leave no doubt that He is the World Teacher. In a worldwide radio and TV broadcast, Maitreya will mentally overshadow all of humanity simultaneously. Each of us will hear His words inwardly in our own language. This is a method of telepathic contact which will reach everyone, and all will know that the World Teacher is now among us.

When this "Day of Declaration" occurs, tens of millions of Aquarians will accept Maitreya as the New Age "Christ." Tens of millions of Christians will believe that he is the Antichrist. What will be the results of this stupendous event? That is why we must prepare now. If Maitreya turns out to be a fraud, then millions of Aquarians will be ready to hear about the real Christ. Christians need to be prepared to witness to them. If Maitreya becomes more than just a fad, or a cult leader, then Christians need to be prepared. I will let the reader decide for himself if this Maitreya is a fulfillment of Bible prophecy as the Antichrist, another New Age charlatan, or just another false Christ.

Who is this "Lord" Maitreya?  What devious plans do the
Aquarian conspirators have for you, your family, and your
country?  What can we do about it?

# 3

# PART THREE

## The Old Age Is Decaying

In the Creme ad, the forerunner of the New Age "Christ" cries aloud against the evils of the world:

> *THE WORLD HAS HAD enough . . . OF HUNGER, INJUSTICE, WAR. IN ANSWER TO OUR CALL FOR HELP, AS WORLD TEACHER FOR ALL HUMANITY, THE CHRIST IS NOW HERE.*

Granted, the world is in sad shape. How so? Take world hunger for example. Seventy percent of children in the Third World countries are suffering from malnutrition. In places like Africa and India, hundreds of millions are suffering a slow and painful torture called starvation. If death doesn't follow soon for them, a crippling life is certain. Millions of babies are born into this wretched poverty each year, and hundreds of thousands of them are born with terrible birth defects caused by the malnutrition of their mothers.

Millions upon this earth know nothing of freedom, but only various degrees of repression, torture, imprisonment, and slavery. The "sweat shops" that blighted some parts of Europe and America a hundred years ago are still doing brisk business in many countries. Communist countries, even under Gorbachev, have institutionalized the "sweat shop" except, of course, for the ruling elite who benefit from the masses. There are perhaps millions undergoing torture in prison camps that still dot the globe. Concentration camps still exist, but now they are quaintly referred to as "re-education camps" and "hospitals."

In this century alone, there have been two world wars and uncountable smaller wars that have taken the lives of hundreds of thousands, and inflicted tragedy on many more. Millions of troops are constantly in training, preparing themselves with terrible chemical, biological, and conventional weapons of war. Our enemies have pointed hundreds of nuclear warheads at our country. These warheads have the capability of destroying this planet many times over. Now the arms race has even expanded into space.

Almost daily, the news media reports the activities of terrorists blowing up planes in flight, killing hundreds of innocent people in public buildings, murdering bus passengers with home made explosives. Terrorist leaders have already publicly boasted that they will make Americans less safe at home than abroad. Some terrorist groups are just a hair's breath away from acquiring atomic capabilities!

Where else has humanity "had enough"? The AIDS epidemic has grown out of control, threatening to make the Black Plague look like a picnic in comparison. In Sub-Sahara Africa, the disease threatens to wipe out a large portion of the population. Adult homosexuals are not the only victims. Many children receiving blood from infected donors have contracted the virus.

In the U.S., people who live moral lives, and receive only sterile blood transfusions, have little to fear. Yet, in Africa, it is becoming commonplace for children to bury both parents because of AIDS.

As we will see later, all of these problems have one thing in common—they are the result of an "evil Christian culture," according to New Age elite. They will, in fact, convince the American public of just that. The evidence the New Agers have amassed to disseminate this propaganda, and their complete control of the flow of information in this country, promises swift and harsh reaction against the Christian community.

The world economic situation has also reached a crisis stage. U.S. banks have loaned out billions to Third World countries to avert their vicious cycles of poverty, hunger, revolution, and untimely death. Many of these countries have defaulted on their loans, and the vicious cycle continues. Default threatens the world economy with collapse.

Is there any good news for humanity? Acid rain is destroying the great rain forests of the North. Pollution may be causing the ozone layer, the protective seal around the earth that screens out deadly radiation, to evaporate into space. Some scientist believe there is a hole in the ozone above Antarctica, and there is evidence it's growing!

Anything else? Race riots in South Africa, religious wars in India and Northern Ireland. In the U.S., child pornography is rampant. Just unfold your newspaper, and you will see a world crying out for help. Who's listening? Christians know that God is listening. He has always listened, and still offers the only perfect plan by which all may live together in peace. The solution is the Gospel. Satan also has a plan. To achieve his evil ends, he offers his plan to the world.

New Age propagandists like Benjamin Creme declare that the world must accept Maitreya as Lord, because he, and he alone, can solve our worldwide problems. Naturally, this Maitreya will not be accepted by a world with many religions and many nations. Therefore, a one-world religion and a one-world government is necessary. Impossible? Over half a billion people on the earth today (New Agers) believe it is very possible!

Who are these New Agers? They are members of the New Age movement—a vast network of organizations dedicated to bringing  about this one-world religion and one-world government (hereafter  referred to as the New World Order). The New Age can mean anything from Amnesty International to Zen Temples. Millions of people each  year are joining its ranks. Why? Because these New Age organizations preach such things as peace on earth, good will toward men.

New Age leaders promise peace and happiness, no more hunger, no more injustice, no more war if only the world unites under the New World Order. Their plan, like Creme's ad, is very attractive. With billions crying out for help, what could possibly "be wrong with wanting universal justice, peace, and prosperity? Nothing could be wrong with this, unless, of course, those doing the promising are lying and have something very different in mind.

Through its tens of thousands of networking organizations, the New Age movement promises to make this world a better place for all. The New Ager presents himself as a knight in shining armor, doing battle with evil forces. What are these evil forces?—Racism, sexism, imperialism, fascism, and materialism—They also proclaim to forefront the effort to abolish war, injustice, and poverty. New Age type groups also lead the anti-nuclear, world peace, and disarmament movements. Other New Age type groups, like Amnesty International, claim to be leading the fight for human rights. New Age type organizations like ZPG (Zero Population Growth), World Hunger, and Planned Parenthood, say they are leading the way to right the wrongs of poverty, hunger, and overpopulation.

New Age leaders tell their immense following that they are the forces of Light in battle with the forces of Darkness. Who are the forces of Darkness? None other, they say, than those that believe in our Judeo-Christian society. They will tell you that the world's present condition is the result of our repressive and narrow minded Judeo-Christian society. Racism, sexism, nationalism, imperialism, and economic exploitation, they say, are all fruits of this society. These wrongs, they tell us, can only be righted when a just society replaces the evil one. What do they have in mind? You guessed it, a New Age society.

What is the New Age society? It is the Aryan-Luciferian Society. This society dates back to the antediluvian (before the Great Flood) era. The Bible informs us that it was a perverse society. So much so, that God destroyed it by a flood. The society that existed then practiced the black arts of magic that included astrology (charting the course of the stars to determine human action), necromancy (communicating with the dead—evil spirits impersonating the dead—for advice), and psychic power. Their holy places consisted of caverns cut into mountains. Out in the desert, when they were away from mountains, they built ziggurats (holy mountains). These ziggurats are similar to the pyramids of Egypt. The ancients constructed caverns in these structures. Near the top, most of them would have a representation of the Zodiac.

The Tower of Babel was one of these ziggurats, probably the first and last truly great one. Genesis tells us that "the whole earth was of one language, and of one speech. And it came to pass, as they journeyed from the east, that they found a plain in the land of Shinar; and they dwelt there. And they said to God, 'Let us build us a city and a tower, whose top may reach unto heaven ...' Moses explains their motive.

> Let us make us a name, lest we be scattered abroad upon the face of the whole earth. And the Lord came down to see the city and the tower, which the children of men builded.

> And the Lord said, "Behold, the people are one, and they have all one language; and this they begin to do: and now nothing will be restrained from them, which they have imagined to do. Go to, let us go down and there confound their language, that they may not understand one another's speech."

So the LORD scattered them abroad from
thence upon the face of all the earth: and they
left off to build the city. Therefore is the name
of it called Babel; because the LORD did there
confound the language of all the earth: and
from thence did the LORD scatter them abroad
upon the face of all the earth. (Gen. 11:4-9)

Here we have a perfect representation of the New Age
movement. All mankind was one, not through the Lord but by
their own effort. The Scriptures tell us how this was done.
Nimrod, we are told, "began to be a mighty one in the Earth.
He was a mighty hunter before the LORD: wherefore it is said
'Even as Nimrod the mighty hunter before the LORD' " (Gen.
10:8-9).

In the Hebrew, this does not mean that Nimrod was a great
animal hunter as might be presumed from the English trans-
lation, but a terrible hunter of men doing evil arrogantly before
the Lord in broad daylight. Such a man was Nimrod who
conquered and enslaved entire nations. He was the epitome of
pride and arrogance. Yes, the world was one, but only by
subjugation. Nimrod was the first world emperor.

In the millennia following Nimrod, others tried to make
the world one. You know their names: Nubuchadnezzar,
Attila the Hun, Julius Caesar, Ghengis Khan, Napoleon,
Alexander the Great, Adolf Hitler, Hirohito, Mao-Tse-Tung,
Josef Stalin. Some of them may appear to be very attractive
and colorful characters in history books, but the fact is these
despots have caused the deaths and suffering of millions of
human beings. Each wanted to make the world one. Each was
kind enough to volunteer himself, of course, as world
emperor.

Why did they build the Tower of Babel, and did they really
believe it would reach the stars? We shouldn't think that they
were unlearned men. They were masterful engineers, scientists and artisans rivaled only in recent decades. Their great
towers were their temples. They did believe they could climb

to heaven but in a spiritual sense—not a physical one. The Tower of Babel was to be a monumental project that would bring great fame to its builders and unite all the peoples of the earth in its grand purpose. The authorities felt that it would have the power to keep the upper castes in awe, and the lower castes in fear. The biblical assertion is clear. These men were attempting to build a "city and a tower whose top is in the heavens; let us make a name for ourselves, lest we be scattered abroad over the face of the earth" (Gen. 11:4).

Do New Age leaders believe they are building a new Tower of Babel? One of the leaders of the New Age movement wrote in a New Age magazine that the spiritual path has "a special connection to the story of Babel since the builders of Shinar (like we of the New Age) sought to build a tower to reach the heavens. In our attempts to transcend purely physical limitations, we too are reaching to the heavens."[1]

Occultists believe that the King of the World is in complete control of this world. This king, they say, dwells in Shamballah. Just under the King of the World, in this spiritual hierarchy, are the Masters of Wisdom. Occultists tell the uninitiated that the Masters of Wisdom dwell in the caverns of Tibet, with their immediate disciples living openly in the world. Supposedly, these Masters of Wisdom direct the affairs for good, and will ultimately cause all nations to be one in love and peace.

To the initiated, the King of the World is Sanat Kumara. You know him as Lucifer. They believe that it is he, Lucifer ("Light-Bearer") who is the "Light" of the world. Who are the Masters of Wisdom who rank just below Lucifer? They are spirit entities who have power over the forces of nature.

Occultists contend that Tibet is sacred because it is where the Masters of Wisdom dwell. The initiated know that the King of the World and the Masters of Wisdom dwell in Shanballah. Where is Shamballah? Occultists tell the uninitiated very little, except to suggest that Shamballah is lost somewhere in the Gobi Desert, or in a hidden valley in Tibet.

The initiated know something different. They know that Shamballah is the region of the hollow earth. The spiritual region where the King of the World and his Masters dwell.

Yes, under the earth's crust, in the physical realm is molten lava. In the spiritual realm, however, it is the region of the spirit entities: Shamballah. Do we find reference to this in the Bible? We do. David wrote in Psalms that "those who seek after my soul, to destroy it, shall go into the lower parts of the earth" (Ps. 63:9). Paul wrote that Jesus, after his death, but before his resurrection, had "descended first into the lower parts of the earth . . ." (Eph. 4:9). Peter wrote that Christ "went and preached unto the spirits in prison" (1 Pet. 3:19). His purpose was to lead "captivity captive" or, in other words, to lead righteous spirits out of hell.

Kwam Yin, a spirit "entity," told New Age Channeler, Pam Davis, about Shamballah:

> Do you not know that the center of your Earth, it is not that which has been spoken by your scientists, the bubbling of the molten rocks, it is beauteous. It is home for thousands upon thousands of Beings that have lived there in totality of harmony and understanding of love.[2]

Who rules in Shaballah? Occultists say it is Sanat Kumara the King of the World. Paul, in the Bible, calls Satan "the god of this world" (2 Cor. 4:4). Just who are his understudies, these Masters of Wisdom? The Bible identifies them as familiar spirits, and warns us in no uncertain terms against accepting their counsel. In fact, we are told to abjure those "that have familiar spirits, neither seek after wizards, to be defiled by them: I am the Lord your God," Isaiah had warned earlier.

> And when they shall say unto you, "Seek unto them that have familiar spirits, and unto wizards that peep, and that mutter": should not a people seek unto their God? for the living to the dead? To the law and to the testimony: If

they speak not according to  this word, it is
because there is no light in then. (Isa. 8:19-20)

Who are the disciples of these Masters of Wisdom? The
disciples are mediums, or channelers, as New Agers prefer to
call then. These channelers tell the uninitiated that they are
communicating with ancient wise men who once lived on
earth and through their superior wisdom can guide us to a
better world. The channelers call upon these spirit entities to
possess them and speak through them.

Christians know that these spirit entities are the familiar
spirits that God warns us against. They are evil beings from
the pit (Shanballah) who "kept not their first estate" (Jude 6).
God cast them out with Lucifer and one-third of the hosts of
heaven. We read about this in the book of Revelation:

> And there was war in heaven: Michael and his
> angels fought against the dragon; and the
> dragon fought and his angels, And prevailed
> not; neither was their place found any more in
> heaven. And the great dragon was cast out, that
> old serpent, called the Devil, and Satan, which
> deceiveth the whole world: he was cast out to
> the earth, and his angels were cast out with
> him. (Rev. 12:7-9)

Lucifer wanted to exalt himself to sit upon God's throne.
God defeated Lucifer; and the Lord cast him, and his angels,
out of his kingdom (Rev. 12:9). How much has pride influenced mankind for evil? How many men have tortured and
killed millions in their quest for personal glory? How many
millions of unborn infants have been tortured and killed by
prideful women? How many have been enslaved for the
benefit of a prideful few? We can see why heaven had no room
for the likes of Lucifer and his cohorts.

A passage from Isaiah tells us that Satan wanted to "sit
upon the mount of the congregation, upon the sides of the
north." What does this mean?  The ancients saw the cosmos
as one great celestial mountain.  At the summit of this heaven-

ly mountain was the North Star. All the heavens seemed to revolve around this star as the earth turned and made its yearly orbit of the sun. Ancient Hebrews and Chaldeans looked upon the North Star as the symbolic Throne of God, the center around which all stars revolved. This was the "sides of the north"—of the heavenly summit.

It was from the top of a mountain that God revealed himself to Moses, and he commanded his prophets to offer sacrifice on the tops of mountains. When the Temple was eventually built, it was at the top of Mount Moriah in Jerusalem. The Temple was where God communicated with his prophets and where God performed the sacred rites that pointed to the coming Messiah.

As the Judeo-Christian community looks to the temple in Jerusalem, so the New Agers look to the Tibetan caverns for their "revelations." Satan has his temples also. Until the children of darkness built their ziggurats, they offered their meditation and occult rituals in the caverns of mountains. The caverns represented Shamballah or the pit. Tibet, to the east of Shinar, had many of these caverns where occultists communed with the Masters of Wisdom. They continue to commune with them to this day.

When men entered the plains of Shinar from the east, they constructed a ziggurat, (an earthly mountain representing the cosmos) and built caverns inside to represent Shamballah. Here is where the occultists practiced the black arts.

Every pagan nation had these types of temples. The Sumerians shaped their temples like the Tower of Babel. In Egypt, they were triangular shaped with the summits pointing directly to the North Star. The Mayans had astrological observatories on top of theirs, and the Aztecs sacrificed some fifty to a hundred thousand human being a year on theirs. The Hindus and Chinese did not have to build ziggurats since the caverns of Tibet were close by. They simply made pilgrimages. Pilgrimages to Tibet are still being made today.

The Judeo-Christian world looks to the Temple at Jerusalem. Jews see the Temple as the site of the coming of the Messiah. Christians believe Jesus will return and rule the earth from the Temple at Jerusalem. Muslims, although they pray facing Mecca, have built their Omar Mosque (Dome of the Rock) on the same site in Jerusalem and expect the prophet Mohammed to return there and reign for a thousand years.

Where do the Aryan-Luciferians (New Agers) look? Not to Jerusalem, but to the caverns of Tibet, where they have had constant communication with the King of the World and his Masters of Wisdom.

After the Great Flood, the Masters gained control of man and once again built a great pagan empire in Babylon. Here is where the great ziggurat or Tower of Babel stood. What does Babylon mean? It means, "the Gate of God." Surely not our Lord, but the "god" of this world. Babylon became the worldwide center of abominations: astrology, necromancy, sexual perversions, to name a few. The Bible makes no secret that the "Mother of Harlots" is Babylon:

> And there came one of the seven angels which had the seven vials, and talked with me saying unto me, Come hither; I will shew unto thee the judgment of the great whore that sitteth upon many waters: With whom the kings of the earth have committed fornication, and the inhabitants of the earth have been made drunk with the wine of her fornication.
>
> So he carried me away in the spirit into the wilderness: and I saw a woman sit upon a scarlet coloured beast, full of names of blasphemy, having seven heads and ten horns. And the woman was arrayed in purple and scarlet colour, and decked with gold and precious stones and pearls, having a golden cup in her hand full of abominations and filthiness of her fornication: And upon her forehead was the name written, MYSTERY, BABYLON THE

GREAT, THE MOTHER OF HARLOTS
AND ABOMINATIONS OF THE EARTH.
(Rev. 17 : 1-5)

## THE ABOMINATIONS OF BABYLON

What were the abominations of Babylon?  They were the
same abominations that Paul prophesied for the last days, and
the same abominations that the New Agers are promoting for
their "perfect" society:

> THIS know also, that in the last days perilous
> times shall come.  For men shall be lovers of
> their own selves, covetous, boasters, proud,
> blasphemers, disobedient to parents, unthank-
> ful, unholy, without natural affection,
> trucebreakers, false accusers,  incontinent,
> fierce, despisers of those that are good, traitors,
> heady, highminded lovers of pleasure more
> than lovers of God; Having a form of
> godliness, but denying the power thereof: from
> such turn away.

> For of this sort are they which creep into
> houses, and lead captive silly women laden
> with sins, led away with diverse lusts, ever
> learning, and never able to come to the
> knowledge of the truth. Now as Jannes and
> Jambres withstood Moses, do these also resist
> the truth: men of corrupt minds, reprobate
> concerning the faith. (2 Tim. 3 : 1-8)

New Age teaching, which is straight from Hinduism,
teaches that man's highest purpose is to transform his own
atman, or self, into God.  Is this not what Lucifer wanted and
still intends to do?  By exalting themselves to become God,
New Agers believe they can be saved from the cycle of birth
and rebirth.  How does one exalt himself to be God, according
to New Age propagandists?  They must follow the Masters of
Wisdom.  What do the Masters teach?  That the only way to
become one with God is to develop one's self. This is done in

various ways, involving yoga, occult rituals, transcendental meditation, etc.

Whatever the method, the result is the same. People begin to concentrate on self more and more. As they develop the natural man: who is an enemy to God, people become lovers of their own selves: covetous, boasters, proud, blasphemers, etc. Their own gratification becomes their constant concern. They do become their own gods.

What is the result of millions of little gods running about? Moral diminution, ethics become situational, and standards are compromised. Anything becomes justified as a means to an end.

What are the fruits of this? Hundreds of billions of dollars in the U.S. alone are stolen each year in stock market swindles all by supposedly respectful people. Perhaps over a million unborn infants are tortured and murdered each year, and this has become socially acceptable. Pornography and even child pornography are ruled harmless by superior court justices. Such abominations as homosexuality, drugs, divorce . . . become acceptable. In fact, all normative rules of conduct become merely matters of taste or opinion. To identify the moral law with reality, or to advance a rational argument in support of an objective morality is, to these people, nonsensical.

Yet New Age leaders have convinced their followers, and many others, that the ills of the world are really the result of our Judeo-Christen society. Going through their whole litany—pointing out "Christian" atrocities of the Dark Ages, present-day racism, sexism, imperialism, pollution, nuclear arms, and all forms of injustice—they lay every bit of it at the door of the Judeo-Christian establishment.

A mind open to the truth can discern that these ills are the direct result of natural man trying mainly to gratify himself. Yet the New Age message, that this "terrible decaying society" must be replaced by the New World Order so that all these

"Judeo-Christian ills" can be abolished is inspiring to many. So far, over a half billion have converted to the New Age Plan.[3]

Just who is really responsible for the world's ills? Let's see.

## *HUNGER*

All the world's hunger problems cannot be placed solely upon Judeo-Christian shoulders. Western nations have the highest standards of living in the world. U.S. exports in 1980 for example, "made up 84% of the world total of corn, 82% of soybean and 45% of wheat."[4] Researcher, Lowell Ponte, wrote in his book *Food: America's Secret Weapon*:

> The United States, with control of over 57 percent of the world's exportable grain, is the Saudi Arabia of food. Only 8 of the world's 173 nations—the United States, Canada, Australia, New Zealand, Argentina, South Africa, France and Thailand" consistently produce significantly more food than they consume.
>
> And among these eight food-producing nations, the United States alone, has a larger monopoly over food exports than all the nations of OPEC combined have over world oil exports.[5]

The West (Judeo-Christian) has little trouble, in feeding itself. What about the East (Aryan-Luciferian)? Lowell Ponte continues:

> But if many countries could move toward self-sufficiency in food if they chose to, there is one major developed nation that seems chronically unable to do so no mater how hard it tries, the Soviet Union. Despite investments sometimes topping $50 billion per year—more than five times what the U.S. government spends

directly on agriculture, the Soviet Union has been unable to feed itself.[6]

New Agers, and other liberals, would be quick to justify such disaster by claiming that "Russian weather is bad." However, this doesn't work. Why? In the Soviet Union there is a "black market" in agriculture. Many peasants grow their own crops in backyards. These crops are worked after their long hard days on the collectives. Peasants then sell the produce from these back-yard crops and keep the profit. Soviet leaders look the other way. Why? Because these "free enterprise" back-yard crops, according to the Russian economics journal *Ekonomicheskaya Gazeta*, produce thirty-one percent of Russia's meat production, thirty percent of milk, thirty-two percent of eggs, thirty-five percent of vegetables, sixty-four percent of potatoes, and fifty-eight percent of fruits! All this on just one percent of the land under cultivation![7]

India is the very heart of the Aryan-Luciferian society. How are they faring? Researcher Tom Anderson in his book *Food for War*, wrote:

> One seventh of the world's population are Indians. One million additional Indians are said to be born every month. Indian farmers plant approximately the same acreage as American farmers and get only forty percent of the yield, over one-third of which is eaten by rats. India has an estimated 2.4 billion rats—Including the Communists—that's five rats for each of the nation's estimated 480 million (1969) people. Most Indians will not kill any living thing, thus rats are "holy." Indians turn more rats loose than even our Supreme Court.

> One-fourth of America's wheat production has been sent to India in the past year— 12 million tons—six hundred ships ferrying a million

tons a month. Indian rats eat more than that.
But the Indian people expect us to feed them
and the rats too. We are hated but the rats are
holy. India is predisposed to socialism—and
its government is pro-Communist. The state
owns and controls practically everything.[8]

India, the Soviet Union, and other Eastern countries have
been deriding America for decades. We are accused of being
selfish, arrogant, and hypocritical imperialists. Those that
have screamed the loudest are fed on American grain. These
leaders can't even feed their own people. The famine in
Ethiopia is a good example. Ethiopia is a Marxist nation, and
when the famine hit, Americans, and other Westerners, dug
deep into their own pockets to help the famine victims. Mr.
Yonas Deressa: president of the Ethiopia Refugee Education
and Relief Foundation (which brought humanitarian aid to
over three million Ethiopians) wrote:

> Under Haile Selassie, Ethiopia usually
> produced enough food not only to feed itself,
> but also to export agricultural products. Under
> the burden of Communist agricultural policy,
> Ethiopia's economy has collapsed: The per
> capita productivity of the peasantry had fallen
> significantly, while the amount of land under
> cultivation has actually decreased. Seven to
> eight million people, still are on the brink of
> starvation, despite good rains and massive
> Western aid. In the cities, nationalization of
> large and small businesses alike has led to
> mass bankruptcies and to an unemployment
> rate of 50 percent and rising. Ethiopia's
> foreign exchange reserves are long gone:
> Mengistu now owes $5 billion to the Soviet
> Union for the arms that have fed a sevenfold
> expansion of the military.

> By now, the Ethiopian regime's role in
> creating the famine has been well documented.

Ethiopia's neighbor Kenya which was hit harder by drought, has experienced none of Ethiopia's mass starvation and disease. The Kenyan government took reasonable and prudent measures to deal with the food shortage. Mengistu, on the other hand took a leaf out of Stalin's book and saw the drought as an opportunity to crush resistance. Not only did he fail to get food to his people—for some time he tried to keep international relief agencies from knowing there was a famine.[9]

While the American people sent bread, the Soviet Union sent bullets. Even with our own droughts and farm failures, the U.S. is still feeding the world. Have New Age prophecies of disaster come true? New Age author Dennis Gabor wrote two decades ago that "it has been estimated that by 1975, the United States will have no surplus of food for export."[10] The secret initiated have tried to fulfill this prophecy, but the hard-working and independent American farmer has defied it. Soon, however, when the farms here in the U.S. are out of the control of independent farm owners, the situation will change for the worse.

Yes, hunger exists in the West, but it is the exception to the rule. In the East, however, hunger and disease are the rule.

## INJUSTICE

All the world's injustice cannot be placed upon Judeo-Christian shoulders. Yes, racism, sexism, and imperialism exist in our Western society. However, these ills can be traced right back to pagan eras and doctrines in India; for example, the Brahmins (Aryans) are treated as gods on earth, while the lower castes are treated worse than animals. Professor John Campbell Oman of Lahore college of India (now Pakistan) wrote of a typical experience when a pariah (lower caste) woman entered a boat with members of the sacerdotal caste (Brahmins):

Watching the passengers disembark from the
ferry-boat, my friend observed a Brahmin run
in an excited manner up to a woman who,
shrinking timidly from observation, was
evidently trying to conceal herself behind the
throng of people who had just left the boat. Off
went the Brahmin's slipper as he reached the
woman and he struck her repeatedly with it;
nor was it till the European had interfered
personally, and forcibly, that he resisted from
this unmanly assault. The victim of the attack
was a pariah woman, who had presumed to
enter the same boat with a man of the sacerdotal caste. That was the serious crime for which
she received public chastisement with the
approval, no doubt, of all Hindu onlookers.[11]

Indeed, in India, temples are dedicated to sacred rats and
monkeys. Millions of tons of food are consumed by "sacred"
rats, monkeys, and cows in temples while millions of "lower
caste" human beings die slow and painful deaths by starvation
in the streets and villages.

## *RACISM*

How does racism compare between East and West? We
have seen that in India racism is gospel. In the West, racism
is opposed to the gospel. Is the Soviet Union a classless
society? Well, the white Russians are only one of fifteen
different nationalities, yet they control virtually everything.
Though white Soviets are becoming outnumbered by
dark-skinned Soviets such as the Kazahks and Tartars, these
dark skinned citizens are curiously absent from government
councils, universities, and better-paying jobs. In the "racist"
West, different races are included in the highest chambers of
government, education, and business.

Nevertheless, the leaders of the New Age, and their
strategically placed sympathizers will soon begin to incite the

public against the Christian community. The Christians will be targeted as the major cause of the inequalities in our society. Controlling the media and the flow of information, the New Agers will make it very difficult for the Christian community to defend itself.

What about the Christian leadership of South Africa? Can racism in that region be blamed on Christianity as the New Agers would like? Hardly, the Nationalist Party took power in 1948. Since that time they have passed all the laws we now call apartheid. The Nationalist Party is still in power to this day.

Slowly, the National Party has been initiating South Africa into the Aryan doctrines of "racial purity." The official symbol of the Broederbond is the Triquetrum. Is it a Christian symbol? Let's see. According to Maureen Stafford and Dora Ware, researchers on symbols, the *Triquetrum* comes from pagan sources: Triquetrum: a primitive device in the form of three radiating axes, associated with the rotary movement of the sun, and having an affinity with the sacred wheel of Hinduism and Buddhism.[12]

Compare these pagan doctrines of "Aryanism" with what it says in the New Age Bible interpretation written by Corrine Heline:

> Man will be emancipated from Race Spirit direction when he has evolved the divine powers within himself to the point where he becomes master of his own course. Seven root races succeed one another in the racial evolution on a planet during a world Period... Aryan [is] the term applied to the Fifth root race.

We cannot find one word about "racial purity" in the Bible. The Bible does not once mention the term "Aryan." However, Hindu and Buddhist scriptures are full of them. New Age writings, which are just modern missionary tracts for Hinduism, are full of them. The Jews copied the pagan practice of "racial purity" when they came back from exile in Babylon.

Jesus let them know what he thought of the idea. He spoke directly to, and drank water offered by, a Samaritan woman (John 4:9). Doing so made him, in the eyes of the Jews at that time, racially unclean. His action even shocked his own disciples. The Master, however, was teaching by example that the doctrine of "racial purity" was a doctrine of the devil.

New Age propagandists are still saying that the Judeo-Christian society spawned the injustice in South Africa. Now you know the truth about the matter. Racism in the West is opposed to the Gospel. Racism in the East is their gospel!

## *SEXISM*

Sexism has been sighted as another of our society's terrible injustices. Can the blight of sexism be placed solely upon Judeo-Christian shoulders? The seething hatred of the Judeo-Christian God by feminists is well documented. Mary Daly, a New Age feminist leader, wrote a paper called "Theology After the Demise of God the Father: A Call for the Castration of Sexist Religion." In it she castigates Christianity for enhancing and perpetuating sexism: "Patriarchal religion has made it more difficult to see through the injustices of the system by legitimating and reinforcing it. The long history of legitimation of sexism by Christianity is by now too well known to require detailed repetition here."[13]

A century earlier feminist leader Elizabeth Cady Stanton would contend, "Take the snake, the fruit-tree and the woman from the Bible, and we have no fall, no frowning Judge, no Inferno, no everlasting punishment—hence no need of a Savior."[14]

Feminists worked hard throughout the past century to convince women that the Judeo-Christian tradition had kept them in bonds long enough. They cried aloud for women to come out of that society, and enter a new one. What would replace the old spirituality? At first Atheism, but naturally, something will have to take its place.

What is it? In 1982 feminists wrote *The Politics of Women's Spirituality*. One reviewer's critique follows:

"Goddess worship, paganism, Wicca, and witchcraft are all names for a form of natural religion that is centered around the mystery, sexuality, and psychic abilities of the female."

Feminists have been screaming for decades that the Judeo-Christian "Father-God" is a terrible and sexist tyrant. Now they are saying that we should look to the East—toward the "goddess" for the new spirituality. A few women decided to look East, but they looked farther and deeper than the feminists wanted them to. One such woman is Professor Denise Carmody. Dr. Carmody looked so far and deep that she looked "beyond the veil" of the new feminist spirituality. In other words, she found the truth of the matter. Women cannot even gain salvation, according to classical Hinduism, until they have "been reborn as men." Dr. Carmody paints a dismal picture of a woman's status in the Hindu culture.

> The most concise index of women's place in classical Hinduism is the traditional common belief that no woman of any caste could gain salvation, except in a future life, when she had been reborn as a man.

> Logically, to be born a woman was the result of bad karma, for it meant that one was ineligible for moksha (salvation) in this samsaric round (incarnation). Tightening women's bind, orthodoxy excluded them from the most prestigious ways of accumulating good karma—study of the Vedas and meditation. Women's salvational discipline (yoga), then, was largely by way of "works." Specifically, she would advance by being a good wife, which meant by exalting her husband. So, one finds injunctions to consider one's husband a god and be his most faithful worshipper.

> The *Laws of Manu* (about 100 CE) instruct women to be loyal, even if their husbands are deformed, unfaithful, drunk, offensive, or

debauched. To ritualize this attitude, or-
thodoxy suggested that the wife adore the big
toe of her husband's right foot morning and
evening, bathing it, offering it incense,
waving lights before it.[15]

Manu, the Hindu Moses, said that "It is the nature of
women to seduce men...."[16] Sadly, Buddhist literature came
to make women an obstacle to monk's perfection and painted
females as sexually ravenous, greedy, envious, stupid, and
generally repulsive.[17]

The reader may be thinking, "If the East treats women so
badly then why do the feminists want the West to be like
them?" What is the answer to the injustice of sexism? Dr.
Denise Carmody gives us a clue:

> In the forth chapter of John's Gospel, we find
> another important indication of Jesus' attitude
> toward women. First, his speaking to the
> Samaritan woman at the well directly and
> courteously both surprises her and amazes the
> disciples. Second, rabbinical teaching of
> Jesus' day held that Samaritan women were
> "menstruant from their cradle"—that is, a con-
> stant source of ritual impurity. By speaking
> with a female heretic, then, Jesus was doubly
> polluting himself. Finally, because she shows
> faith and honesty, Jesus makes this woman a
> herald of his message to her village, where
> many came to believe in him. He was no
> respecter of conventional taboos.
>
> Jesus treats men and women simply as
> individuals who need his help, or as co-
> workers, or friends. He offers women no
> separate but equal way of works; he
> compiles no segregating list of feminine
> virtues. ...When Jesus cured without concern
> for the hemorrhaging woman's ritual purity, or
> broke the Sabbath law of rest to heal a woman

(Luke 13:10-13), or exorcised the evil spirit from a woman's daughter (Luke 7:2-10), he showed himself to be free of the law on women's account, as much as on men's. Since women were definitely second-class citizens in the Judaism of Jesus' time, his democracy was quite striking.[18]

The Apostle Paul wrote that "Nevertheless neither is the man without the woman, neither the woman without the man in the Lord" (1 Cor.11:11). Paul admonished husbands to "love their wives as their own bodies" (Eph. 5:28). Paul continues:

> For this cause shall a man leave his father and mother, and shall be joined unto his wife, and they two shall be one flesh. This is a great mystery: but I speak concerning Christ and the church. Nevertheless let every one of you in particular so love his wife even as himself; and the wife see that she reverence her husband. (Eph. 5: 31-33)

In the Judeo-Christian tradition, the husband and wife are one unto the Lord. They are two equal halves, together making a whole being. Paul tells them to love and respect each other accordingly. Christian women are to love and reverence their husbands, and their husbands are to love their wives as themselves (meaning to reverence their wives). What a contrast this is to the debased "slaves" of the New Age. What is the answer to solving the injustice of sexism? Jesus.

## *WAR*

New Age propagandists point out that our present Old Age society has spawned war mongering devils like Adolf Hitler. They say we must change our society into a New Age one—thereby bringing peace and safety to the world. What they don't tell you, and the uninitiated among them don't know, is that Adolf Hitler was an occultist—well versed in the writings of Theosophy founder Helena P. Blavatsky. *Secret Doctrine* is the title of her major work. Dietrich Eckart, Hitler's mentor, writes of the Fuhrer, "He will dance but it is I who will call the tune! I have initiated him into the SECRET DOCTRINE, opened his centers of vision and given him means to communicate with the powers."[19]

Before making any move, Hitler would consult his astrologers. Imagine the surprised Russians when they entered Berlin and discovered the Holy Men of Tibet. More than once, Hitler sent expeditions to the "sacred" caverns of Tibet. According to Gerald Suster author of the book *Hitler: The Occult Messiah*, a close associate of Hitler, named Rauschning, later wrote of him that one "cannot help thinking of him as a medium . . . beyond any doubt, Hitler was possessed by forces outside himself . . . of which the individual name Hitler was only the temporary vehicle." Author Joseph Carr, in his book *The Twisted Cross*, says that "one cannot argue against the claim that the Nazi world view and major elements of the New Age movement are identical . . . for they both grew out of the same occult root: theosophy."[20]

Hitler belonged to two occult groups: the Vril Society and the Thule Geselschaft. Aryanism's triumph was their main goal and both originated in India. The members of these occult societies "took irreversible vows in service to Lucifer" says Trevor Ravenscroft in his book *The Spear of Destiny*. Many Hindu leaders to this day still openly praise Hitler. One of them, the Swami Svatantrananda, declared, "Whatever you may say against him, Hitler was a mahatma, almost like an avatar. He did not eat meat, he did not have intercourse with women, he never married, and he was the visual incarnation of Aryan polity."[21]

Everyone knows that the Nazi symbol was the Swastika, but few know where it comes from. As Elisabeth Goldsmith, in her *Ancient Pagan Symbols* suggest: "The Swastika is a Sanskrit word composed of *su* good and *asti* being, with the suffix *ka*, and is the equivalent of 'It is well,' or 'So be it.' It was reverenced in India three thousand years before the

Christian era. . . . It was used before the Aryans commenced their migrations, and has been called the oldest Aryan symbol."

Why did the West develop nuclear arms? Because Hitler was well on the road to developing them. He had his scientists working around the clock to produce the first atomic bomb. Hitler forced the U.S. into the nuclear arms race. Had we refused the challenge, he would have likely enslaved the world.

Another close ally of Hitler, Fascist Japan, was busy depopulating China, reigning with terror in the Philippines, and bringing death, destruction, and terror to half the globe. Why? So that the world would be forced to worship a little god named Hirohito. With the infamous, and totally unprovoked, massacre at Pearl Harbor, the U.S. entered World War II. While Christian ministers in America prayed for peace, Buddhist and Shinto (both New Age) priests in Japan prayed to their gods for the glory of their emperor! Can New Age propagandists really hold our Judeo-Christian societies culpable for the carnage and calamity of these wars?

The Fascists leaders in Japan told their people that the Americans were devils, and that death was better than the fate they would receive if they surrendered to the Americans. So, when Japanese-occupied islands were taken, American soldiers would witness Japanese parents throwing their children from cliffs and then going over themselves. Those sinful gods in Japan were determined that they would wedge a mountain of the dead bodies of their own people between themselves and the advancing U.S. forces.

Leaders knew that if they invaded Japan, millions of innocent Japanese would die uselessly for their emperor not counting the millions of U.S. casualties. By this time the U.S. had developed the bomb. Right or wrong, they decided to use the bomb. U.S. leaders thought it was better that tens of thousands should die to save the lives of tens of millions.

We dropped the bomb on Hiroshima. The emperor refused to surrender. We dropped a second bomb on Nagasaki, and the emperor still refused to surrender. U.S. forces then told the emperor that the third bomb had his name on it. The emperor immediately called for a full unconditional surrender! Thus ending World War II.

The U.S. was, because of the bomb, the most powerful nation that ever existed. America, if she had simply wanted to, could have easily conquered the entire planet. She alone had the bomb. What did she do? Instead of conquering the world, she rebuilt her enemies countries until they were better than before. She fed the world. She established peace. However, the Aryan-Luciferian society was still alive and well. The Soviet Union was still there, and peace would soon be gone. What about the Dark Ages, and the Inquisition? Wasn't that a product of the Judeo-Christian society? Let's see.

## THE DARK AGES

The Dark Ages were a terrible time. For the most part, ignorance, death, disease, injustice, and war marked that age. However, there were times when justice, science, liberty, and righteousness prevailed—eventually culminating in the Renaissance. New Age propagandists have been using the Dark Ages as an example of what would happen if the Judeo-Christian society had full reign. They say we must become a New Age society, or we'll sink into the Dark Ages again. Nothing could be further from the truth! The superstitions of the Dark Ages cannot be imputed to Christianity but rather to the barbaric Germanic tribes who invaded civilization. The Dark Ages were influenced by mysticism, a "New Age" mysticism. In the Dark Ages kings practiced astrology. Professor Henry S. Lucas writes that, "Astrology, which teaches that the stars influence terrestrial affairs, is of ancient origin, either Chaldean or Egyptian. It was appropriated by the Greeks and Romans...and during the close of the Middle Ages, especially in the fourteenth century, it appears to have been accepted almost universally."[22]

Most people are unaware of the fact that during the Dark Ages, if a man was found reading the Bible, he could be burned alive. It was the job of Christianity to climb up out of the darkness and superstition of that period and move events toward the Renaissance. Many reform movements sprang up during the Dark Ages. Many Christians were tortured and killed by horrible means because they advocated such "heresies" as reading the Bible.

New Age propagandists would have you believe that the Dark Ages was a period when Christianity reigned. The truth is just the opposite. The Masters reigned then. When the people began to turn again to the Bible, and reject the sacramental occultism of that period, a rebirth occurred: the Renaissance. The Masters want revenge! It is they who want to bring us back into the Dark Ages.

New Age leaders tell the uninitiated that the Old Age has brought the world to a point where total destruction can come at any time. They say that we must all accept the New Age to survive. They tell us that we must accept the New Age "Christ" as Lord; only he can assure us, they say, that there will be no World War III. Yes, the world has had enough! It is ripe for the same con game Satan has used from the very beginning! The Masters will use the uninitiated New Ager. Now they flatter people and coax them in with promises of peace and justice. They teach doctrines that appeal to the natural man in us all, and then , after they have used us, they will send us to our destruction. In the next chapter, we'll look at the modern New Age movement, name some names, and see just how they plan to put their "Lord Maitreya" into world power.

# 4.

# PART FOUR

# Preparing The Public For Lord Maitreya
## *THE MODERN TOWER OF BABEL*

**B**enjamin Creme, the New Age "Prophet," announces the coming of the "Great World Teacher" in his ad: *THE CHRIST IS NOW HERE*.

New Age leaders and propagandists declare that the world (meaning the Judeo-Christian world) is old, decaying, and dying. They say that it must be replaced by a New World Order, a New Age. They declare that they are working for this New Age, when all the nations of the world may be one. They contend that our present old world cannot bear this, because of religious, racial, and national differences, which are, they say, the root causes of hunger, injustice, and war.

To alleviate these conditions, the New Age propagandists tell us, the world must become one: religiously, socially, economically, and politically. How could this possibly come about? There is a plan. In this chapter we'll review the history of the modern New Age movement and take a look at this plan for a modern Tower of Babel.

The roots of the modern New Age movement can be traced back to Helena Petrovna Hahn Blavatsky, called "HPB" by her followers. She was born on July 30, 1831, in the town of Ekaterinoslav in Russia's Ukraine. She was born to an aristocratic blue-blooded family. During her early adult years, Spiritualism (communication with the dead) had gained wide acceptance among the world's elite. She became a very popular medium (today we call them "channelers").

At a young age she married General Nikifor Asilievich Blavatsky. However, the marriage did not last. Helena was too "free spirited,"and engaged in many affairs during her worldwide travels.

Her journey into the occult became deeper and deeper. She traveled to the occult centers of the world: Egypt, Tibet, etc. In 1858 she traveled to France and became an associate to the famous medium (channeler) Daniel D. Home. In 1871 she founded the Spiritualist Society. Embroiled in fraud, the society folded quickly. In 1873 she met Henry Steele Olcott, with whom two years later she formed the Theosophical Society. In 1878 the Society moved to Adyar, India, its stated purpose being to oppose the Christian missionary movement there. One Society brochure stated their objective in India this way:

> To oppose the materialism of science and every form of dogmatic theology, especially the Christian which the Chiefs of the Society regard as particularly pernicious; to make known among Western nations the long-suppressed facts about Oriental religious philosophies, their ethics, chronology, esotericism, symbolism; to counteract, as far as possible, the efforts of missionaries to delude the so-called 'Heathen' and 'Pagans' as to the real origin and dogmas of Christianity

and the practical effects of the latter upon
public and private character in so-called
Christianity.[1]

In other words, the Society attempted to countervail
Christianity and promote paganism (New Age Theology).
Blavatsky had a special altar erected at the Society headquarters in Adyar, where she claimed to receive messages from
the Masters. She wrote an entire library of books based on
messages from the Masters with a commentary on the
messages.

The Society grew. Charles W. Leadbeater, a Liberal
Christian in the Anglican priesthood, joined the Theosophical
Society in 1883 and soon became one of its chief propagandists. Leadbeater could have become Blavatsky's successor,
but in 1906 the authorities charged him with promoting sexual
deviation to some young boys in his care. The Society tried
to defend him, but he had to be overstepped as heir of the
Society because of the bad publicity.

Blavatsky claimed to be in frequent contact with the
Masters who were aged but youthful looking men who lived
in Tibet. The Master Koot Hoomi was a frequent
communicant with HPB. She described him as "tall,
handsome, benign," who would give words of counsel and
then vanish into thin air. During her travels she made
thousands and thousands of converts to the Society.

In 1884 a scandal broke loose in the Society. Blavatsky's
biographer, John Symonds, tells us what happened:

> In 1884, the founders returned in triumph to
> Europe. Lady Caithness, Duchess of Pomar,
> entertained them at her palace at Nice, and
> while the colonel was in England lent Mme
> Blavatsky a flat in Paris. The most exalted
> French mystics made their pilgrimage to her.
>
> She came over to England where the Society
> for Psychical Research proposed that they
> should investigate her . . . But before they had

time to publish their conclusions, a bombshell exploded in the very center of Theosophy in Madras.

The Protestant missionaries had published some highly indiscreet and revealing letters, allegedly written by Mme Blavatsky to Mme Coulomb, which clearly exposed the great Mme Blavatsky as a fraud and her 'marvelous phenomenon' as the work of confederates, of whom Mme Coulomb was the most important.

The letters had been brought to the editor of the Madras Christian College Magazine by Mme Coulomb in a rage: she had been expelled from the headquarters at Adyar after a quarrel with other members of the committee in charge. News of the scandal was published in the world's press; it made the Society for Psychical Research reconsider their not unfavorable views on Theosophy. The crudeness of the relations startled them. Mme Blavatsky it was alleged, had got Mme Coulomb to make a dummy figure of a man that on moonlit nights Mr. Coulomb wore on his shoulders to give the faithful the impression that it was Koot Hoomi hurrying by. And Mme Coulomb had described how she had dropped the Mahatma letters through a slit in the rafters. . .

The Society for Psychical Research sent an Investigator, Richard Hodson, to India to find out what he could and report back. And after him, hurriedly, followed Mme Blavatsky to sue the missionaries for libel. These Coulomb letters were entirely forgeries, she declared.[2]

Once back in India, however, the Society found that the Christian missionaries refused to recant under threat of legal suit. In fact, they "had been patiently waiting for her to attack."[3] The missionaries said that they wanted to get the Master "Koot Hoomi in the witness box."[4] The trial for libel against the missionaries was set. The Christians had witnesses there, and they were ready. What did Blavatsky do? Symonds says Mme Blavatsky fled back to Europe, never to return to India.

The Society for Psychical Research at last issued their report. In it they described Mme Blavatsky in terms that have helped to keep her memory green but which at the time she did not find flattering. "For our own part," they said, "we regard her neither as the mouthpiece of hidden seers, nor as a mere vulgar adventuress; we think that she has achieved a title to permanent remembrance as one of the most accomplished, ingenious, and interesting impostors of history."[5]

We shouldn't think that HPB never spoke to her Master Koot Hoomi. It's possible that she did. However, we must remember that there are uninitiated New Agers and initiated New Agers. The initiated know the truth regarding the occult teachings. The uninitiated know only what the initiated tell them, which are lies and veils set in front of their eyes. Why? So they can be "prepared" (slowly) for the "higher truths"!

The initiated "truth" is that Master Koot Hoomi is a spirit entity that possesses the body of the medium. HPB was the "vehicle" that "Master" Koot Hoomi entered into and possessed. Yet, the initiated tell the uninitiated that the "Masters"(including Koot Hoomi) are living men that dwell and work in Tibet. Since Koot Hoomi could only "possess," and not materialize, HPB had to concoct a phoney "appearance" of Koot Hoomi in order for the uninitiated to see that he was real. The initiated knew better. Christians know that "Master" Koot Hoomi is an evil spirit that possesses the bodies of mediums, or channelers. Yes, Koot Hoomi is real. He is not an aged man living in Tibet, but an evil spirit from the pit.

## ANNIE BEASANT

Probably Blavatsky's greatest disciple was Annie Besant. She became president of the Society at Blavatsky's death in 1891. Born Annie Wood, in London, England, in 1847, she married Frank Besant in 1867. In 1874 she met atheist freethinker Charles Bradlaugh, and joined his *National Secular Society*.

Ann Besant's skills as a writer promoted her to co-editor of Bradlaugh's humanist journal, *The National Reformer*. In 1876 they formed a publishing company together, but the authorities tried and convicted them of publishing pornographic literature. Annie became well known for her feminism and advocacy of birth control. During the 1880's she entered a relationship with humanist George Bernard Shaw, and she soon joined his Fabian Society (the Socialist Movement of Great Britain). A few years later she deserted her husband Frank.

In 1888 someone gave her a copy of *The Secret Doctrine* by HPB. Besant immediately became a disciple, and soon an initiate. She travelled around the world at Blavatsky's request, for the promotion of the Theosophical Society. The years that followed were busy ones for her. Besant wrote and spoke for the cause of Theosophy everywhere.

At Blavatsky's death in 1891, Henry Olcott claimed that he had received a message from the Masters declaring that Besant must become the new leader of Society. She accepted, and the society grew in popularity. During the next two decades, Annie Besant began to talk of the coming of a great avatar (incarnation of a god). This next avatar, she said, would be a "great world teacher" who would lead the world into its next stage of evolution.

Then in the winter of 1908/09, a society member in Adyar named Narayaniah asked the society to care for his motherless boys, among them Krishnamurti Jeddu. Leadbeater cared for these boys, but was particularly attached to little "Krishna," as he was called. Leadbeater worked tirelessly developing the lad's "psychic powers." Gregory Tillett, Leadbeater's biographer, describes him and his periodical *The Buddhist*:

> *The Buddhist* contained many instances of Leadbeater's newly acquired dislike of Christianity. In one issue, expressing his delight that the Buddhist festival of Wesak was being properly celebrated in Ceylon, he noted that it was unlike religious festivals in England. These were "bestial orgies, savage combats and brutal horseplay, and defiling the balmy air with volleys of oaths and indecent language." And in speaking of the increasing number of converts to Christianity he described it as "the progress of perversion." Since the teachings of this "perversion" was neatly summarized in the Catechism of the Church of England, Leadbeater expressed his contempt of them by burning a Catechism at a meeting of the Galle Branch of the TS [Theosophical Society]. The incident acquired some notoriety, and it was rumored that he had in fact burned a Bible, declaring it to be a "pack of lies."[6]

Leadbeater, with Annie Besant, soon became convinced that Krishnamurti was the body to be used by the new avatar for his appearance. Besant wrote a letter to Leadbeater further admonishing him to "prepare" the boy for the possession, "so it is definitely fixed that the Lord Maitreya takes this dear child's body. It seems a very heavy responsibility to have to guard and help it, so as to fit in for Him, as He said, and I feel rather overwhelmed, but we are together in it and your wisdom will illuminate."[7]

Late in 1909, Besant formed the Order of the Star of the East; to promote her belief that Jesus, as Lord Maitreya, had returned in the person of Krishnamurti. Over the years, young Krishna was being primped and primed for his role as the New

Age Christ. Leadbeater was put in charge of Krishna's "spiritual development" by the Masters.

There was a series of court battles initiated by Krishnamurti's father. He brought child sexual abuse charges against Leadbeater, and desperately tried to win custody of his sons back from the Society. Leadbeater and Besant placed delay after delay before the court, but it finally came to trial. Some of Narayaniah's (Krishnamurti's father) witnesses were impressive. They included some of Leadbeater's former close associates.

Narayaniah claimed that when he had first heard of the "irregularities" between his sons and Leadbeater, he demanded that Leadbeater not be allowed to see or be near them again. He said that Annie Besant assured him that "the boys would be separated from Leadbeater."[8] Instead of separating the boys, however, Besant moved them in with Leadbeater. Narayaniah claimed that in spite of this, they were again being allowed to associate with the said Leadbeater, and it was "about this time that [I] heard from other Theosophical friends that one Luxman, a personal attendant, had seen C. W. Leadbeater and Krishnamurti in the defendants room engaged in committing an unnatural offence."[9]

The main defendant in this custody trial was, of course, Leadbeater. He was charged with "committing sodomy" with his pupils, and of "engaging in mutual masturbation" with them. "Besant, who had no small influence over the rich and powerful of India, took the stand for Leadbeater. His biographer, George Tillett, comments:

> There were . . . a few things which might have led the suspicious to wonder. Why did Leadbeater invariably sleep with a young boy in his bed? And why did he invariably have a boy in the bath with him? It has been argued that his weak heart necessitated such companionship for fear he might have some sort of attack alone; but does companionship require mutual nakedness in close proximity? And

why did Leadbeater insist on communal bathing for his pupils at The Manor, with all of them in the bathroom, naked, at the same time? He was given an enema every morning by one or other of his pupils, in the presence of the others whilst they bathed.[10]

It is no wonder why Leadbeater despised Christianity and the Bible with a seething hatred. Both condemned his perverse abuse of young boys.

The judge in the custody case ruled for the plaintiff, Narayaniah. The court criticized Leadbeater as having "immoral ideas," and they believed him to be "a highly dangerous associate for children."[11] However, for some unexplained reason, the court did not pursue criminal charges against Leadbeater. During his years with Blavatsky, Leadbeater had written several articles for her periodical. The subjects were on adult responsibilities and relationships with children!

The official magazine of the Theosophical Society was called *Lucifer*. In its first issue (Sept/Feb, 1887), Blavatsky defends the name *Lucifer*, "If one analyzes his rebellion, however, it will be found of no worse nature than an assertion of free-will and independent thought . . . meaning no worse than 'light-bearer' (from lucis, 'light,' and ferre 'to bring')."[12] In the New Age (Hindu) doctrine of Maya, we all create our own reality. We become our own gods: independent thought and action. Doesn't this sound appealing? It didn't sound very appealing to the six million Jews who were tortured and killed because Hitler, and his occult chiefs, independently "thought" them out of existence. What "free-will" did they have when they were led to the gas showers and furnaces? What "free-will" and "independent thought" did the young boys have when they were forced upon by "His Holiness" Leadbeater? New Age leaders want millions of these gods ruling the planet, bowing down only to themselves, and their "Lord" Maitreya

Besant and Leadbeater left India for a European tour, and with them Krishnamurti. He was now eighteen, and, under

law, was free to go where he chose. He chose to follow Besant
and Leadbeater. Before they left India, however, they rushed
Krishna through the final stages of initiation. They took him
to the "sacred" caverns. There he "met" the Masters of Wisdom. Krishna described it in these words:

> When I left my body the first night, I went at
> once to the Master's house and I found Him
> there with the Master Morya and the Master
> Djwal Kul. The Master talked to me very
> kindly for a long time, and told me all about
> the initiation, and what I should have to do.
> Then, we all went together to the house of the
> Lord Maitreya, where I had been once before,
> and there we found many of the Masters—the
> Venetian Master, the Master Jesus, the Master
> the Count, the Master Serapis, the Master
> Hilarion and the two Masters Morya and K.H.
> (Koot Hoomi). The  Lord Maitreya sat in the
> middle and the others stood round Him in a
> semi-circle. Then the Master took my right
> hand and the   Master  Djwal Kul my left,
> and they   led me in front of the Lord
> Maitreya. . . .The Lord smiled at me, but He
> said to the Master: "Who is this that you bring
> before me?" And the Master  answered: "This
> is a candidate for admission to the Great
> Brotherhood . . ."

> Then the Lord turned away from me and called
> towards Shamballah:   "Do I this, O Lord of
> Life and Light, in Thy name and for Thee?"
> And at once the great Silver Star flashed out
> over His Head and on each side of it in the air
> stood a figure—one of the Lord Guatama Bud-
> dha and the other the Mahcohan. And the Lord
> Maitreya turned and called me by the true
> name of my Ego, and  laid His hand upon my
> head and said: "In the name of the One

Initiator, whose Star shines above us, I receive you into the  Brotherhood of Eternal Life."[13]

The Society hailed Krishnamurti as the new avatar. Their message was proclaimed boldly throughout the world that "The Christ Is Now Here." The elite of Europe, very "liberal" at that period right before the rise of Hitler, was steeped in mysticism, spiritualism, mesmerism (hypnotism), socialism, and occultism. They accepted Krishnamurti with open arms. Krishnamurti, and his Theosophical Society chaperons, left Europe triumphant and sailed for America.

The aristocracy in the U.S. were less "liberal" than their European cousins, and the masses were, almost to the man, Judeo-Christian. The *New York Times* reported on Krishna's arrival in America . . .

> The World Teacher's spirit has taken posses-
> sion of the young Indian, Krishnamurti, the
> same spirit that occupied the body of the man
> Jesus. Mrs. Besant said today: "Several times
> the World Teacher has used the appointed
> vehicle. The moments of actual possession are
> becoming more and more frequent and will
> shortly be permanent." Krishnamurti has now
> reached the stage, his followers say, where he
> is able to leave the carnate body at will and
> commune with the World Teacher in occult
> regions.[14]

Upon entering New York harbor, Krishna began to act peculiarly. He seemed to be going through a state of withdrawal. Christian researcher and author Dave Hunt commented on this oddity in the following: "As his ship pulled into New York harbor, Krishnamurt's occult powers suddenly and mysteriously left him. He had come to America to oppose historic Christianity, particularly its teaching about sin, repentance, judgment, and forgiveness through the death and resurrection of Jesus the Messiah . . ."

It seems that Krishnamurti's spirit guides had left him. The *New York Times* reported that Krishnamurti became almost incoherent during an interview aboard ship. Instead of manifesting any miraculous abilities, he came off as "a shy, badly frightened, nice looking young Hindu."[15]

What caused this "god on earth" to turn into a stumbling bumbling teenager? In Europe he spoke with superhuman intelligence, and his demeanor was one of startling power. In America, however, he could barely finish a sentence. Was it the "electrical currents" of New York City? Was it the prayers of a Christian America who had read of the coming of the "Great World Teacher" to their shores in their newspapers?

Krishna soon renounced himself as the New Age "Messiah." He also renounced the Theosophical Society. He did return to his father, and his father's brand of Eastern Mysticism. He became a very popular writer and lecturer in mystic circles, probably because of his former notoriety. His books can still be found today at New Age bookstores. In their maddening effort to get Krishnamurti away from his father, and Indian courts, a second time, Besant and Leadbeater acted too quickly.

It is believed by many that the Lord Maitreya did take possession of Krishnamurti's body, but the vehicle (Krishna himself) was unable to handle the entity. Why? There seems to have been too much "negative Karma" in the American tour. In other words, the American masses just weren't ready for the "Lord" Maitreya. Actually, America, at that time, was still a God-fearing, praying nation. It is possible that the satanic spirit that possessed the boy had to flee! The Society had failed the Masters, but they weren't going to let that happen again. The next time, America was going to be ready. Leadbeater was demoted. Annie Besant was soon replaced, but not without a struggle from Alice Bailey.

## ALICE BAILEY

Alice La Trobe Bateman was born in 1880 in England. As a teenager she served as a Sunday school teacher. One Sunday morning, she was stunned to see the door to her home open and a tall stranger with a turban walk in and speak to her. This turban-headed stranger told her of a great work that she had been called by the Masters to perform. Over the next decade she was to have a number of bizarre psychic experiences. Eventually she travelled the world, only stopping when she reached the Theosophical Society headquarters in Pacific Groves, California.

Theosophy appealed to her with its doctrines of reincarnation, a Hierarchy of masters, and karma. Once at the Society, she observed a picture of the Master Koot Hoomi, a spirit entity that communicated with Blavatsky and Besant, and Alice immediately recognized him as the turbaned man who spoke to her years before. In the Society, Alice met and married Foster Bailey, a fellow Theosophist.

In 1919, Alice was approached by a Master, Djwal Khul (He is referred to as "D.K."), who declared that he was to become her control in the telepathic transmissions of a series of books. What is contained in these books? The plan for a New Age. This New Age, of course, could only be brought about with the advent of the New Age "Messiah" (Lord Maitreya). To encourage the advent of this "Christ," meditation groups were set up to help channel the energy from the Masters. Each group or person is seen as a "point of light" radiating the mystical powers.

A particularly effective way of channeling is the use of the Great Invocation, a meditation prayer revealed through Alice Bailey. It is repeated through Alice Bailey. It is repeated slowly and with solemnity while one visualizes the pouring down of power from the Masters. The Great Invocation reads:

> From the point of Light within the Mind of
> God, let light stream forth into the minds of
> men.  Let Light descend on Earth.  From the
> point of Love within the Heart of God, let love
> stream forth into the hearts of men.  May
> Christ return to Earth.  From the Center where

> the Will of God is known.　Let purpose which
> the Masters know and serve.　From the center
> which we call the race of men.　Let the Plan
> of Love and Light work out.　And may it seal
> the door where evil dwells.　Let Light and
> Love and Power restore the Plan on Earth.

To understand what this "prayer" means, we must first understand just what New Age teaching is. What is it? Paganism. A good example of modern paganism is Hinduism.

## THE RELIGION OF BABYLON

What is Hinduism? The casual student of the religions of India will become immediately dumbfounded at what appears as the enormously complicated mass of doctrines, philosophies, and practices of Hindus. The more experienced student will see that Hinduism isn't really complicated at all because a good description of it is found in the Bible.

The Bible warns us against the Hindu practices of astrology (Deut. 4:19, 17:3; 2 Kings 17:16; Isa. 47:3; Zeph. 1:5, etc.), necromancy (Lev. 20:27, Isa. 28:7, 1 Chron. 10:13, 2 Chron. 10:13,33:6, etc), nature worship (Judges 3:7), and the immoralities that accompany these practices.

The Religion of Babylon, as described in the Bible, was concentrated in the worship of Baal, the Baalim, and the Great Mother (called by the Hebrews, Ashtaroth).

## THE MASTERS

What does "Baalim" mean? It means the "Masters." Just as there is a divine Christ, there is an Antichrist. Christians are aware that below God, in the divine hierarchy, there are seven archangels, or spirits, as described in the book of Revelation. In the hierarchy below Satan, there are seven archdemons, or Masters. They are Master Meon (Num. 32:18), Master Peor (Num. 25:3; Deut. 4:3), Master Perazim (2 Sam. 5:20), Master Shalisha (2 Kings 4:42), Master Tamar (Judges 20:30), Master Zebub (2 Kings 1:2), and Master Zephon (Ex. 14 : 2): these are the Baalim ("Masters").

In Theosophy, the names are Sanat Kumara, and under him are the seven Masters: Master Morya, Master Koot Hoomi, the Venetian Master (Djwal Kul), Master Serapis, Master Hilarion, Master Jesus (not the real Jesus, but Apollonius), Master Prince Rakoozi (also known as Master the Count). We are sure that these are just other names for the very same archdemons, and Satan himself.

Sanat Kumara, with the help of these Masters, according to New Age propagandists, desires only the welfare of mankind. Godhood, the ultimate goal, can be only brought about after mankind has evolved from his now spiritually immature state, to a higher state of consciousness. There are seven levels of consciousness, each one higher than the other and closer to Sanat Kumara. These seven levels are 1) Physical, 2) Astral, 3) Mental, 4) Institutional (Buddhic), 5) Spiritual (Nirvanic), 6) Monadic (Anupadaka) and finally, 7) Divine (Adi).

The purpose of life, the occultists say, is to reach the highest plane or level of consciousness. This can't possibly happen in one lifetime, so we are constantly going through a cycle of birth and rebirth, given lifetimes to reach higher planes of consciousness and enlightenment. It is no coincidence that the ziggurats of Mesopotamia are seven tiered; each tier higher than the first (paintings and drawings of the Tower of Babel give a good description of this).

Here we have man trying to exalt himself to Godhood. The Self becomes the object of a man's worship, and the result of such worship is the worship of Satan. The sin of Lucifer was pride for saying in his own heart, "I will ascend into heaven, I will exalt my throne above the stars of God: I will sit also upon the mount of the congregation, in the sides of the north: I will ascend above the heights of the clouds; I will be like the Most High" (Isa. 14:13-14). Jesus, the only good Master, said, "Neither be ye called master: for one is your master, even Christ.

Over the years, Alice Bailey worked on her writings. The next step was to form a publishing trust so that her channeled messages from the Master could be propagated. In the early 1920s the Bailey's formed the Lucifer Publishing Trust. This name, quite appropriate for their cause, did, however, create some unwanted publicity. They changed the name from Lucifer Trust to "Lucis" Trust. The name "Lucis" meant the same thing, but with the revised name the Bailey's could avoid the unwanted publicity.

In time, the writings became disseminated among people and groups opposed to the Judeo-Christian Society. Soon, people began to form special interest groups dedicated to one or the other New Age cause. Eventually people began to network—meaning they would share resources, information, meet together, etc.

In the 1960s, there was a major attempt by the New Age groups to establish an Aryan-Luciferian Society in the West. As usual, they preyed upon the young, for the young were impressionable and easier to control and deceive than adults. They were called the "Hippie" generation.

This was the time of the "sexual revolution." Mankind lost that revolution. Teenage pregnancy, divorce, adultery, immorality, and finally AIDS, have won—hands down. This was the time of "The Beatles," each with his own guru straight from India. This was the time when hundreds of thousands in this country became "turned-on" to drugs. Now, hundreds of thousands cannot be "turned-off" (often, no matter how hard they try), and their lives are being destroyed.

Were the Masters successful in establishing an Aryan-Luciferian Society here in the West in the 60s? No, but in the 90s the answer may change. The Masters are determined not to fail again!

The Soviet Union leads the world in parapsychology (the study and development of psychic phenomenon). Russians spend astronomical amounts of money each year in the area of psychic research, money which could have gone to feeding its hungry peasants. They have dozens of institutes dedicated to this pseudo-science. New Age doctrine has appealed to millions of atheists, who then become New Agers.

Many scientists are now "rediscovering" God because the physical universe has, they say, the scientific stamp of a creator. It was the scientists who said a hundred years ago that the universe came about at random, with no "unseen intelligence" behind it. Now, they are finally admitting that all the evidence points to a creator. New Age propagandists, some of whom are scientists themselves, are striving in a series of publications (such as The Tao of Physics, God & The New Physics, etc.) to make sure that the "god" science is discovering in nature will be Lucifer.

Karl Marx never disbelieved in God; evidently, he just hated Him. Then why was the "God is Dead" movement conceived and promoted? First, it was a plan to convince the world that there was no God at all. Secondly, when man has no higher power to be accountable to, he worships himself. His own needs, gratifications, and lusts become his gods. Once this is achieved, man is prepared for the final stage—the introduction of New Age theology.

What is New Age theology? Your SELF is God! For the atheist, who has been worshipping his own self already, calling self "God" is a very easy and natural step. Christian author and apologist (Defender of the Faith) Norman Geisler comments on how the New Age is bringing back the old pagan gods:

> Polytheism is not just a primitive pagan belief that ancient cultures held. It is enjoying a widespread revival today, even in America. This growing phenomenon was noted by David L. Miller, Associate Professor of Religion at New York's Syracuse University, in his 1974 book *The New Polytheism: Rebirth of the Gods and Goddesses*. He argues that, since God has "died" in Western society, there is no longer "a single center holding things

together. . . . The death of God has given rise
to the birth of the gods."[16]

As we see, the atheistic or "God is Dead" movements were
not ends in themselves, but ingeniously developed and ex-
ecuted conspiracies to "dethrone" the Only True God, and
replace him, in the minds of mankind, with Lucifer and his
demonic hosts (the pagan gods).

What is the next step in bringing about this New Age
society? We see it everyday. Everything from the emergence
of Satan worshipping cults, to backward masking by Satan
worshipping rock bands, to humanistic education in public
schools, to deceptive ecumenical movements within our own
churches. What resistance will Christians, or Jews and orthodox Muslims for that matter, meet when they try to protect
themselves and their children from being subtly initiated into
the New Age? New Age propagandists have warned of the
fate of those daring to resist their "Shamballah" force. I can
assure you, they are deadly serious.

# 5.

# PART FIVE

## How Will We Recognize Maitreya?
### THE MAGICAL YEAR

The Creme ad gives us a few clues:

*Look for a modern man concerned with modern problems—political, economic, and social. Since July, 1977, the Christ has been emerging as a spokesman for a group or community in a well-known modern country. He is not a religious leader, but an educator in the broadest sense of the word—pointing the way out of our present crisis. We will recognize Him by His extraordinary spiritual potency, the universality of His viewpoint, and His love for all humanity. He comes not to judge, but to aid and inspire.*

Before we can identify the New Age "Messiah" in part 6, we must first know his marks of identification. In addition to Creme's own clues, we will draw upon other material to identify him. In attempting to point him out, we can pull together information from his own disciples, from Christian writers and researchers on the New Age movement, and from the Bible. Going in that order, let us press on.

The expectation of a Great World teacher, a promised "Messiah," meeting the needs of all world religions was first promoted, as we have stated, by Helena P. Blavatsky. She declared that she was receiving careful instructions on this from the Masters. After her death, Annie Besant and Charles W. Leadbeater promoted their young ward, Krishnamurti, as the expected Maitreya.

Not that Krishnamurti was Maitreya himself—he was not—but the evil spirit that possessed his body. Besant and Leadbeater had rushed Krishnamurti away from his father and Indian courts thus causing Krishnamurti to be unprepared fully for the possession. That, coupled with the negative "karmic vibrations" of the American tour (a still fundamentalist Christian America) spelled failure for this possession.

In 1948, almost two decades after Krishnamurti had renounced his messianic role, Alice Bailey, the new head of the Theosophical Society, published a book entitled *The Reappearance of the Christ*. Bailey argued in the book that the time was ripe for the appearance of a Great World Teacher who would come as both Son of God and head of the Spiritual Hierarchy (the Masters of Wisdom, or Lords of Shamballah).

Bailey suggested that the preparatory work for the appearance would begin in 1975. This is keeping with Blavatsky's "orthodox" view. Besant and Leadbeater had actually "jumped the gun" with the announcement of Krishnamurti. Alice Bailey went back to the Masters' original plan under Blavatsky. HPB wrote:

> Maitreya is the secret name of the Fifth Buddha, and the Kalki Avatar of the Brahmins-the last MESSIAH who will come at the culmination of the Great Cycle . . .

> He will appear as Maitreya Buddha, the last of the Avatars and Buddhas, in the seventh Race. Only it is not in the Kali yug, our present

terrifically materialistic age of Darkness, the "Black Age," that a new Saviour of humanity can ever appear.[1]

In other words, Maitreya cannot take the reigns of a world in the "Black Age." Is the West in a "Black Age"? We must remember that, to the New Age Initiate, white is black and black is white: evil is good and good is evil. HPB was saying that our Judeo-Christian Society must be turned into an Aryan-Luciferian one; then, and only then, can Maitreya appear. The New Age "Christ" must have a forerunner: someone to prepare the way. When will this happen? HPB said this will occur in 1975.[2]

The year 1975 was to be "The Magical Year." In 1975 Benjamin Creme, a Scottish-born student of Bailey's teachings, began to proclaim the imminent appearance of the Christ. Creme first announced his expectations in London, and traveled throughout Europe and to North America. He claimed to have contacted the Spiritual Hierarchy in 1959, and later received instructions to begin his mission of publicity announcing Maitreya's appearance.

One of the most accurate and objective chroniclers of Creme's odyssey is religious historian Dr. J. Gordon Melton, who wrote the following:

> During the 1970s according to Creme, Maitreya materialized a human body into which he incarnated. In 1977 he flew from Karachi to London and took up residence in the Indian-Pakistani community in London, where he began to speak regularly to audiences numbered in the hundreds. On April 24-25, 1982, through advertisements taken out in a number of the world's prominent newspapers, Creme announced that Maitreya's "Day of Declaration" would occur within two months. Followers expected it on or before June 21, 1982. When the Declaration failed to occur and Maitreya failed to appear, Creme blamed

the apathy of the media (a sign of general human apathy). He also announced that the Day of Declaration was still imminent though no new specific date was set. In the meantime, the followers were urged to continue their main task of announcing that Christ is in the world and soon to appear.[3]

In her book, *The Hidden Dangers of the Rainbow*, Christian author and researcher Constance Cumbey has also chronicled the life of Creme. She notes Creme's estimation of the "Christ":

> When Benjamin Creme, spokesman for the so-called Maitreya the Christ, spoke in Detroit on November 4, 1981, he was asked if he had ever met the Christ. His answer was revealing. He said, "No, I've never met the Christ, but I've met the human body he is inhabiting several times—but never as the Christ." This reveals the real nature of the Antichrist and the power behind the New Age movement in general. It constitutes nothing less than old-fashioned demonic possession. The person who will eventually be the Antichrist and consequently the chief spokesman for Satan will be an adult who freely and voluntarily decided to assume the spirit of Satan.[4]

Creme simply teaches that Maitreya is the Christ who is to "possess" a human being. He further teaches that Jesus himself was similarly "possessed." He believes that Jesus is a "disciple of Christ and made the great sacrifice of giving up his body for the use of the Christ. By the occult process of overshadowing, the Christ, Maitreya, took over and worked through the body of Jesus from the Baptism onwards."[5]

New Age leaders and propagandists claim that this "Lord" Maitreya will be the Promised Messiah of all religions. Cumbey continues:

"In order to appeal to Christians, New Agers say Maitreya is the Christ. For Moslems he is the Imam Mahdi. For Hindus he is Krishna."[6]

Christian author and researcher Texe Marrs agrees that Maitreya is appealing to the nations as the "Promised One" of all the great world religions. Marrs asserts:

> Lola Davis (New Age propagandist) identifies the New Age "Christ" as "the One for whom all religions wait, called Lord Maitreya by some in the East, Krishna, Messiah, Bodhisat-va, Christ, Imam Mahdi." She promises, he "will bring new revelations and further guidance for establishing the World Religion ..." According to Davis, until this great avatar or leader returns to earth, it is man's responsibility to "create a new global society that will welcome a World Religion for the New Age." Furthermore, she suggests "... that we assist his earthly and heavenly helpers prepare humanity to recognize and receive him joyously and appropriately whether he be called Lord Maitreya, Buddha, Messiah, Christ, or Immam Mahdi."[7]

In other words, New Age leaders and propagandists, acting under the direct or indirect orders and guidance of the Masters, wish to create a New World Order; this order would include a One World Religion, a One World economic system, political system, etc. How can this possibly be done? To answer that, we must first understand the One True Christ: Jesus of Nazareth, and the concept of Messiahship.

## CHRIST VS. ANTICHRIST

The term "Christ" is an Anglicized version of the Greek word Christos—"The Anointed One." The Hebrew word for "Anointed One" is Messiah. Both the high priest in the Temple and the King of Israel were called the Lord's "anointed," because they were chosen and set apart by the Lord. The high priest was chosen to be a mediator between God and his people, and the king was chosen to be the ruler of the people.

The Lord also called his servants, the prophets, his "anointed"; for they were the voice of the Lord to the people. Hence, the anointed of the Lord were the prophets, priests, and kings of the people. At times the prophets would rule, at times the priests, and at other times the kings. In the time of King David, there was established in Israel for the first time, and the last, the offices of prophet, priest, and king. Israel grew and prospered, righteousness reigned, and peace flourished.

However, the Baalim would not let this last long. Through flattery and lies, they made Israel feel that they could worship Ashteroth and the Baalim along side of Jehovah. The Lord, through his spokesmen the prophets, made it perfectly clear that this wasn't possible. The people, oftentimes already seduced by the deceiving spirits, listened to their false teachers and killed the prophets. They refused the protection and wisdom of the Lord, and bowed the knee to Baal. What they soon discovered is that Baal does not take care of his own, but purposely leads them to destruction.

The only time Israel prospered in the land is when they adhered to the word of God through the prophets, and rejected the seductive evil spirits (the Masters). When the offices of prophet, priest, and king functioned according to God's will, the people prospered. But, those officers were mortal. Many a king would fall and take his people with him, because of his own self-indulgence, self-pride, self-conceit, and self-worship. Not a few priests would fall because of self. At least one prophet (Baalam) fell because of self. The false prophets, priests, and kings believed in the religion of *self*. The people listened with itching ears to the promoters of self-worship, and they killed the true prophets.

The righteous looked for a day when God would send his divine "Anointed One"—a perfect prophet, priest, and king. Only a sinless one could judge sin, and only he could rule justly—without *self*-interest. Prophets foretold of this perfect prophet, priest, and king. They called him the "Anointed One": God's Messiah. Here are just a few of the prophecies concerning Him:

1) A new star will appear at His birth (Num. 24:17).

2) He will be born of a virgin (Isa. 7:14).

3) He will be a descendant of David (Ps. 132:17).

4) He will be born in Bethlehem (Micah 5:2).

5) He will work miracles (Isa. 42:7).

6) He will enter Jerusalem riding upon a donkey (Zech. 11:13).

7) He will be pierced in both hands and feet (Ps. 22:16).

8) He will be given vinegar to drink (Ps. 69:21).

9) His bones will not be broken (Ps. 34:20).

10) He will suffer for other people's sins (Isa. 53:9).

11) He will be killed for the sins of the people (Dan. 9:26).

All of these prophecies, and many more, as we saw earlier, have been fulfilled to the letter in the person of Jesus of Nazareth! Satan, the great imitator, has also sent his own prophets, priests, and kings upon the earth. He also will send his "anointed one" upon the earth, not to save, but to *destroy*.

What does "Maitreya" mean? It is a Sanskrit word meaning "merciful One." The world's Buddhists expect the coming of the Fifth Buddha, a Messianic figure in whose coming they are waiting. The Bodhisatva simply refer to the coming one of the Hindu's Kalki. The Muslims expect the return of Jesus, who is to destroy the Antichrist and reign in righteousness. The Shiite Muslims expect the Imam (Leader) Mahdi (Rightly Guided) to be another Jesus. The Jews, of course, expect the Messiah. The Christians expect the Messiah, Jesus of Nazareth, to return.

All these different and contending religions will, at the advent of their particular Messiah, turn the reigns of government over to him. If there came a man who could prove that he was the Messiah of all these religions, then that would give him power over most of the earth. Is this so bad? Yes, because he would by lying.

The Christ of the Christians, the Messiah of the Jews, and the Imam Mahdi of the Muslims are all the same individual: Jesus of Nazareth. The "Lord" Maitreya of the Buddhists and the Kalki of the Hindus is a different individual altogether. The Master of Jesus is God the Father. The Master of Maitreya is Satan. One is Christ, and the other Antichrist. One is Jesus (Salvation), and the other is Apollonius (Destruction). Jesus will return in his own resurrected body—showing his wounds for those that disbelieve him. Apollonius is dead, but the evil spirit that possessed his body has possessed another in these last days. His forerunner is at this moment announcing his arrival upon the earth from the pit.

## BENJAMIN CREME—THE FALSE PROPHET?

Early in the '70s Christian author Hal Lindsey wrote *The Late Great Planet Earth*. That book opened the eyes of millions to the Bible, and its exact prophecies. In chapter 9 of that book, Lindsey discusses the "False Prophet":

> When John the Baptist, one of the greatest prophets of all time, first saw Jesus coming toward him, he said, "Behold, the Lamb of God that takes away the sin of the world" (John 1:29 NASB). In this statement he summarized the whole significance of the Old

Testament. It all pointed to Jesus. So we see who will worship the Antichrist. Everyone will worship him who has not put his faith in Christ. It is possible for a moment to project our thoughts toward that time when the entire world will look upon one human being as the supreme leader. The Antichrist will need a lot of help to carry out his schemes. His staunchest ally will be The False Prophet. In Revelation 13:11-13 we are introduced to this infamous character. This person who is called the second beast, is going to be a Jew. Many believe he will be from the tribe of Dan, which is one of the original progenitors of the nation of Israel. The False Prophet (he is called that in Revelation 19:20 and 20:10) will be a master of satanic magic. The future False Prophet is going to be a devilish John the Baptist.[8]

In my quest to identify the New Age Messiah, I at first believed that I had hit a brick wall when it came to Creme since he is a Scot. I then discovered that he is Jewish on his father's side. His father was a Russian Jew who immigrated to Scotland. What about Creme being of the Tribe of Dan? Jews are of the Tribe of Judah, not Dan. "How," I asked myself, "can Creme be of the Tribe of Dan when the tribe is among the "lost" tribes? Then I made a startling discovery!

There is an occult doctrine called "Anglo-Israelism." It is held by occultists—and some fringe Christian groups—that the lost tribes of Israel (which included Dan) migrated through Europe to Great Britain and Ireland. Let me say forthright that I do not believe in Anglo-Israelism. Yet, I asked myself, "How can the false prophet be of the Tribe of Dan when the tribe doesn't exist anymore?" Obviously, the false prophet will claim to be a Jew, and of the Tribe of Dan. Occultists (esotericists) like Creme could do this, and this would fulfil Biblical prophecy. We already know that Creme is the son of a Russian Jew (Lindsey calls Russia the land of Magog.) Creme is also a Scot.

What do the Anglo-Israelites say about the Scots? One of their main propagandists, B. de W. Weldon, wrote in his book entitled *The Evolution of Israel*:

> The North was inhabited by two peoples: the Scots and the Picts. The Scots originally came from Ireland, and may have had some connection with the famous Tuatha de Danaan and the Tuatha de Danaan may have had some connection with ancient colonies of Dan. . . . Dan represents modern Scotland.[9]

Another Anglo-Israel work, called *Dan: The Pioneer of Israel*, was written by the Royal-Keeper of the Crown Jewels, Col. J.C. Gawler. In the book he gives page after page of "evidences" that the Danites are now the Scots. This is generally accepted as "gospel" truth among occultists. What about Lindsey's statement about the false prophet being a "devilish John the Baptist"? Glenys Roberts, a reporter for *The Shropshire Star* (a British newspaper published in Wellington), interviewed Creme and his wife. She wrote:

> "How would you feel if your husband woke up one day and announced he was John the Baptist?" That is more or less what happened to Phyllis Creme, a perfectly rational 39 year-old lecturer in communication styles at North London Polytechnic, whose 59 year-old husband, Ben, has taken on the mantle of the wandering prophet.

(The Shropshire Star, II May 1982) She titled her article "The latter day John the Baptist"

Could Benjamin Creme be the false prophet? What is Creme saying? We have already reviewed much of what he had to say. Here, Creme writes on various important subjects. "People have been led to leave the churches in large numbers," he says as he castigates the notion that Jesus is the only Son of God, "because the churches have presented a picture of Christ impossible for . . . thinking people today to accept as the One and Only Son of God . . ." What else does Creme have to say on:

· *The New World Order*—"Already certain Masters are making forays into the world from Their retreats. . . . They can thus directly lay the foundations of the new world order."[10]

· *Apollonius*—"In his next incarnation, as Apollonius of Tyana, Jesus became a Master."[11]

· *Mystery Religion*— "The Ancient Mysteries will be restored, the Mystery Schools reopened, and a great expansion of man's awareness of himself . . . Man will come to realize himself as the Divine Being he is . . ."[12]

· *Antichrist*—"It is not a being, not an individual. It is preparing the way. It is the destructive force of God Himself, which prepares the way for the Christ."[13]

· *Karl Marx*—"Marx was indeed a member of the Hierarchy. . . . Man is one, That, essentially, is what Marx is saying. Man is One, Humanity is One. Eventually, all social systems will tend toward a system which encourages that brotherhood or Oneness of man which Marx senses, as a spiritual being."[14]

· *Women's Lib*—"Women's liberation is a manifestation of a very specific and serious Hierarchical intention."[15]

· *Redistribution of Wealth*—"There is a group of high Initiates, industrialists, economists, administrators, of great experience and achievement who, with Hierarchy, have worked out plans and blueprints which will solve the redistribution problems of the world, when the political will is there to implement them."[16]

*The Great World Teacher*—"All the great religions hold before humanity the idea of a further revelation which will be given by a future Teacher or avatar. Christians hope for the Christ's return, the Buddhists look for the coming of another Buddha, the Lord Maitreya, while the Muslims await the coming of the Imam Mahdi, the Hindus, the Bodhisattva or Krishna, and the Jews the Messiah. Each of them expects a Coming One, a Revealer of new Truths and a Guide into the future. Esotericists know them all as one Being, the World Teacher, the supreme Head of the Spiritual Hierarchy of Masters, and look for His imminent return now as we enter the Aquarian Age."[17]

What is Creme saying here in these examples? He derides the Atonement of Jesus, promotes the New World Order, says that Jesus' "next" incarnation was as Apollonius (which is quite impossible—even with reincarnation—since both men were born at the same time), advocated the return of the Babylonian Mystery Religion, declared that Hitler and other Fascists were part of the "destructive" force of God himself, called Karl Marx a member of the hierarchy, promoted women's lib, and advocated a major "redistribution" of wealth now being planned by unnamed conspirators in high places.

Creme also says that esotericists ("occultists") have been looking and waiting for the advent of the *Great World Teacher*, one claiming to fulfill the expectations of the Messiah for all religions. We shall introduce that figure in the next chapter. First, however, we need to know more about Creme and the Tara Center.

Only a month after Creme's great announcement about the coming "world Teacher," N. W. Hutchings, editor of *The Gospel Truth* (part of the Southwest Radio Church Ministry) did an article on Benjamin Creme and his "Lord" Maitreya. Hutchings points out that almost all religions "have a forerunner" for their promised messiah. He finds it interesting that "Creme contends that he has been called to prepare the way for Lord Maitreya. . . ." Hutchings said, "This is a ploy of Satan to deceive the world . . ."

Other articles in Tara publications call for the redistribution of the resources and wealth of the richer nations—taking from the have's and giving to the have not's. They fail to explain that once the have's have been de-materialized, and the have-not's have used up their portions, there will be no one to produce. Perhaps that will be the time when all the world will have to take the "mark of the Beast" in order to work, buy and sell (Rev. 13).

After listening to Creme at a news conference, Dave Hunt described him as the perfect spellbinder, the man with the most believable, satanic, cosmic message for the world today. Recently, on the "Merv Griffin Show," Creme held his host's attention for ten minutes—to the extent of committing that unforgivable TV sin of passing over a commercial.

In all this, including the miracles and great wonders that he proposed, Benjamin Creme would certainly be a type of the false prophet mentioned in Revelation 13:11-14:

> And I beheld another beast coming up out of the earth; and he had two horns like a lamb, and he spake as a dragon. And he exerciseth all the power of the first beast before him, and causeth the earth and them which dwell therein to worship the first beast, whose deadly wound was healed: And he doeth great wonders, so that he maketh fire come down from heaven on the earth in the sight of men, And deceiveth them that dwell on the earth by the means of those miracles which he had power to do in the sight of the beast...[18]

## *THE TARA CENTER*

The New Age organization that promotes Creme's appearances throughout the world is called The Tara Center. We've already seen how Creme identified "Tara" as the name of the Great Mother. John, in the book of Revelation, called her the "Great Whore."

She is known as Tara in Tibet, Diana and Athena in Greece, and Ashtaroth to the Hebrews. The Canaanites, and often the Israelites, who followed in their abominable practices would sacrifice their children to the goddess. This included blood sacrifice and cannibalism. She is known as Gaia, or "Mother Earth." She is called "Mother Nature." She is cruel and heartless, demanding blood to replenish herself. She is known as Kali in India. She has no right to be called a mother.

Tara has another significance. Though publicly denied by Creme and his followers, the term Tara has connections to Celtic pagan practices. Christian author and editor N.W. Hutchings continues:

> The history of Tara extends back in time many centuries before the O'Hara Estate in the movie, *Gone With The Wind*. According to the *Encyclopedia of Mythology*, by Robert Graves (pgs. 331, 332), Tara, a Hindu goddess and wife of Brihaspati, bore an illegitimate son by another Hindu god, Soma. The child was so handsome and intelligent, that both the husband of Tara and her lover claimed him as their son. Maitreya, who supposedly was born 2,600 years ago, can be identified with the illegitimate son of Tara. Therefore, it is not surprising that the Tara organization is proclaiming him to be the messiah. The legend of Tara and her god-like son was incorporated into other religions, and became the basis for Druidism. Tara Hill, located in central Ireland, was a center for Celtic-Druid worship

(*The Celtic world* by Barry Cunlifte, pages 170,171; *The Celts* by Gerard Herm, page 254). Druidism and the worship of Tara became synonymous with the appearance of the Illuminati movement under the guise of the Masonic Lodge. *The Encyclopedia Britannica* provides this information: *"Druids, United Ancient Order Of, a friendly society founded, as an imitation of the ancient druids, in London in 1781. They adopted Masonic rites and spread to America. . .and Australia.*

Throughout Benjamin Creme's statement concerning Maitreya, and also in Tara's publications, Illuminati terminology is common. The guiding and controlling influence behind Maitreya is declared to be a "Spiritual Hierarchy," identified as the "Masters of Wisdom," the illumined ones. According to Creme, one of the "Masters of Wisdom" has advised him to declare Maitreya, as the Christ. In the printed interview with Creme that appeared in the May 10, 1982, edition of the *Los Angeles Herald Examiner*, Creme is reported as saying: ". . . I have been in rapport with one of the Masters of Wisdom for many years. I was first contacted by him in early January 1969, and over the last nine years prepared by him and trained by him. . . . the Masters of Wisdom are really the disciples of the Christ (meaning Maitreya), The Masters of Wisdom make up a group of very advanced, involved, illuminated and, from all points of view, perfect men . . ."

One of the symbols used in Tara publications is the Illuminate pyramid with the all-seeing eye. The myth promoted by Creme and these "Illuminated Ones," is that Antichrist has already appeared in the form of Hitler, and others. He explains that Antichrist is really the destructive power of God, working to eliminate everything that needs to be destroyed in order for the true messiah, Maitreya, to make his appearance. *The Encyclopedia Britannica* comments on the Illuminati: "A short-lived movement . . . founded on May

Day (May 1) 1776 by Adam Weishaupt . . . a former Jesuit."
The members of this secret society called themselves "perfec-
tibilists." Their founder's aim was to replace Christianity by
a religion of reason. While it is generally reported in reference
books that the Illuminati began in 1776, the movement has
been traced back to the Druids at the time of Christ, and even
further back to Egyptian and Oriental mysticism, the second
millennium B.C.; Therefore, evidence would indicate that this
attempt by the Masters of Illumination to bring forth a messiah
is not new, it can be traced all the way back to Satan in the
Garden of Eden when he enticed Eve to eat of the fruit of the
tree of knowledge, or wisdom.

Whether Mr. Creme will be successful in deceiving the
world into worshipping this man as the "Christ" remains to be
seen. There are certainly some aspects of the bold movement
that coincide with the Antichrist of Revelation.[19]

The Illuminati was a secret organization founded on May
Day, 1776. It is interesting to note that May Day is still the
chief pagan holiday. It is also the one and only official holiday
in Communist countries. We see much more about the Illuminati in the second book in this trilogy: Antichrist
Conspiracy.

## IS MAITREYA THE ANTICHRIST?

There is a growing controversy concerning whether or not
"Maitreya" is the Antichrist. The Christian Research In-
stitute, a cult-watching organization based in Southern
California, came out with this statement:

> Many Christians have been understandably
> disturbed by the striking similarities between
> Creme's description of Maitreya's coming
> reign, and popular contemporary interpreta-
> tion of biblical prophecy concerning the
> kingdom of Antichrist. Indeed, in our opinion,
> it would be unwise to treat these similarities as
> though they had no eschatological (end-times)
> significance.[20]

Christian researcher N.W. Hutchings concurs: "Maitreya . . . is more noteworthy than others recent attempts [candidates] because of its [his] universal scope. . . ."

In an interview by Jack Kisling that appeared in The Denver Post for Sunday, March 21, 1982, Creme makes a startling admission. Kisling asked Creme, "Won't the advent of a single world religion annoy the hierarchies of all the current orthodox religions?" Creme replied, "More than that—they will be shocked, I daresay they will be among the last to accept the New Age." "But," Creme said confidently, "it will come anyway, because it must—we will begin to live as potential gods!"[21] Does this sound familiar? It should, if you read your Bibles, because this was the very thing that Lucifer said in the Garden of Eden:

> And the serpent said unto the women, "Ye shall not surely die: For God doth know that in the day ye eat thereof, then your eyes shall be opened, and ye shall be as gods, knowing good and evil." (Gen. 3:4-5)

Is this "Lord" Maitreya the Antichrist? Christian researcher and best-selling author, Texe Marrs, gives his opinion on the matter in his *Dark Secrets of the New Age*:

> Whether he comes as the Lord Maitreya, as the reincarnated Buddha, Immam Mahdi of Islam, or as another "divine being," the question Christians surely must ask about the coming New Age "Christ" is, is he the Antichrist prophesied in Revelation 13, in the Book of Daniel, and elsewhere in the Bible? My own answer is, Yes, the man for whom the New Age waits will almost certainly be the Antichrist.[22]

## IDENTIFIABLE MARKS OF MAITREYA

We have come to the point now where we must look at the identifiable marks of Maitreya. Since Benjamin Creme is his forerunner, it is natural and logical that we turn to him for hints of his identity. Here are some of the main clues:

· *Maitreya is in London*: Maitreya, the Christ, has been in London since July 1977. He lives as an ordinary man concerned with modern problems.[23]

· *Maitreya is a spokesman for a Pakistani-Indian community in London*: He has been emerging as a spokesman for the Pakistani-Indian community there.[24]

· *Maitreya is the Promised One of All Religions*: All the great religions posit the idea of a further revelation to be given by a future Teacher. Christians hope for the return of the Christ, the Buddhists look for the coming of another Buddha (the Lord Maitreya), while Moslems await the appearance of the Imam Mahdi, the Hindus a reincarnation of Krishna, and the Jews the Messiah. Students of the esoteric tradition know these as different names for one and the same individual, the World Teacher, the head of the Spiritual Hierarchy of Master, and they look for his imminent return.[25]

· *Maitreya uses a common Moslem name*: He does not call himself the Christ or Maitreya, but is living for the time being as an ordinary member of the Asian Community using a common Moslem name.[26]

· *Maitreya's dress*: He varies his headgear and clothes to suit the occasion, sometimes Moslem, sometimes Western. I understand he frequently wears local Moslem costume.[27]

· *Only a few in Maitreya's own community know his true identity*: He himself has said that while there are those in the group in which he dwells who do know his true status, he is withholding his identity for the time being so that he can appeal to us simply as an ordinary man.[28] Those with whom he lives know who he is and are sworn to secrecy. They are close disciples.[29]

· *Maitreya's native tongue*: I have never attended any of his lectures. Since most of the meeting is in Bengali or Urdu, I would not have understood much, either.[30]

We see from Creme that Maitreya is in London, a spokesman for a Indo-Pakistani community, claims to be the World Teacher, uses a common Muslim name, dresses in the local Muslim costume (wears Western clothes on occasion), and speaks Benjali and Urdu (the official languages of East and West Pakistan). Only a few in the community in which he associates know his true identity, and they are sworn to keep his identity a secret.

Creme now tells of an "Asian gentleman" who saw Maitreya in person. Here we are given a description of their Lord: "The Asian gentleman who gave me this information described the man in very similar terms to the journalist who saw Maitreya at a Brick Lane restaurant last year: 'tall, slim, dressed in white Pakistani clothes, broad-shouldered, long face, long nose, high cheekbones.' "[31]

Using sources from Creme himself, including newspapers articles and interviews, we can retrace some of the recent steps of Maitreya. He flew from Karachi, Pakistan, to London, England, in July of 1977. Since that time he has been emerging as a spokesman for a Pakistani community in London. He speaks both Pakistani dialects: Benjali and Urdu. He goes by a "common" Moslem name, and wears the "local" Moslem Pakistani dress. Creme says, as we saw earlier, that Maitreya's plane trip fulfilled the biblical prophecy of Jesus "coming in the clouds" (i.e., the plane descended from the clouds of the sky as it landed in London).

Creme was once asked if Maitreya ever attended morning prayers at a mosque (a Muslim place of worship). Creme replied, "He has occasionally done so in order to become known and seen as one of the community—an ordinary man."[32]

All of this tells us something. Creme may be giving out more "hints" than he knows. He is saying that Maitreya belongs to a Pakistani Muslim community in London, and that Maitreya has been emerging as their spokesman. Creme says that the coming of Maitreya, as he has, would be a terrible heresy to "fundamentalist" Muslims. Obviously then, Maitreya is a member of a London Pakistani Muslim community that does not identify itself as "fundamentalist." How do the Muslims fit into this "New Age" scenario?

## THE MUHAMMADAN CONNECTION

According to Creme, Maitreya appears to the world, at least for now, as an "unorthodox" Muslim. Why a Muslim? Could it be a fulfillment of Bible prophecy?

During the Middle Ages they were called the "Muhammadans"—meaning the followers of Muhammad. Their religion was called Muhammadanism. Christian scholars have debated about Muhammad for centuries. At first they called him Antichrist. At other times, he was a fallen prophet. In recent times, some Christian scholars have suggested that Muhammad was a believer in Jesus, but that his successors, the Caliphs, twisted his message into what we now know as Islam.

Whatever the origin of Muhammad, it is certain that by the time the Caliphs took power, there was no question as to their motives. What were their motives? To destroy Christianity. During the Middle Ages the Turks controlled and ruled the huge Muslim Ottoman Empire. Protestant Reformer Martin Luther vividly portrayed what he believed to be the "two chief enemies of Christ" in his book *On War Against the Turks*.

Both the Protestants and the Catholics were calling each
other the Antichrist, and to prove it they compared each other
with the Turk (Muhammadan).

Christian author Uriah Smith remarks on the Caliphate
and the empire they ruled:

> That religion is Mohammadism, and the Sul-
> tan is its chief minister. The Sultan, or Grand
> Signior, as he is indifferently called, is also
> Supreme Caliph, or high priest, uniting in his
> person the highest spiritual dignity with the
> supreme secular authority...His name. In
> Hebrew, "Abaddon," the destroyer; in Greek,
> "Apollyon," one that exterminates or destroys.
> Having two different names in two languages,
> it is evident that the character, rather than the
> name of the power, is intended to be repre-
> sented. If so, in both languages he is a
> destroyer. Such has always been the character
> of the Ottoman government.[33]

All one has to do is remember the rising tide of
anti-Americanism and anti-Christian fervor that has been
sweeping the Muslim world in recent decades. Fanatical Muslim terrorists have killed many innocent Christians and Jews.
Are they "fundamentalist" Muslims? No, they are not. The
Humanist (New Age) media tries to present these Muslim
fanatics as fundamentalist; however, once again, nothing
could be further from the truth.

Probably the best known "Muslim terrorist" is the Colonel
Muammar el-Qaddafi of Libya. He finances, trains, and
protects thousands of international terrorists. Egypt's late
president Anwar el-Sadat (assassinated by men with Libyan
connections) called Qaddafi "a madman." Sadat was a
Muslim. Another Muslim, the leader of the Sudan, Gaafar
al-Nimeiri, said that Qaddafi "has a split personality, both of
them evil."[34]

After terrorists brutally murdered eleven Israeli athletes in the Munich olympic games, Qaddafi staged a heroes welcome for the surviving assassins, and gave them ten million dollars. This is not all, Qaddafi has his hands bloodied in literally thousands of terrorists acts around the globe. The U.S. Intelligence services uncovered and stopped hundreds of planned massacres here in the U.S. alone. His terrorists activities did diminish appreciably after Reagan bombed Libya.

The American media, overwhelmingly liberal, has been calling Qaddafi and his thugs "fundamentalist" Muslims. Are they?

I still didn't know what Creme meant regarding Maitreya as an "unorthodox" and "non-fundamentalist" Muslim. Then I remembered something I read in Constance Cumbey's *Hidden Dangers of the Rainbow*. What she wrote proved to be very helpful. She said:

> Was Maitreya coming to inaugurate a New Age of peace and light? Or was he coming to inaugurate a reign of terror? The answers are contained within the Alice Bailey writings. Creme had recommended *The Externalization of the Hierarchy* by Alice A. Bailey. I must confess it was an excellent source of information! I learned that the New Age Movement was at its esoteric core profoundly anti-Christian, anti-semitic, and even anti-Moslem (orthodox Moslem, that is-not Sufism).[35]

Every esotericist (occultist) knows what Sufism is. The Sufi is basically a New Age Initiate in Muslim clothing. Martin Lings, a scholar on Sufism, writes:

> The Koran affirms that the community of Mohammed is "a middle people" and it is, above all, in its mysticism that his religion shows itself as a bridge between East and West. A Vedantist [Hindu], a Taoist or a Buddhist can find, in many aspects of Islamic

mysticism, "a home from home," such as he could less easily find in Christianity or Judaism. [36]

The name "Sufi" comes from the Arabic word for "wool." Beginning in the time of the Caliphs there appeared a group of gurus who "infiltrated" Islam. They wore wool: hence the name sufi. James Robson, another noted scholar writes:

> The Sufi Path has for its goal union with God, and some Sufis have uttered what orthodox Moslems consider as blasphemy. A notable example is the saying of al-Hallaj, "I am the Truth", for which he was crucified in 922. There are sometimes suggestions of pantheism, especially connected with the doctrine of the Oneness of Being which teaches that God is the only absolute reality. [37]

To say that we are divine, or to called everything "God" is utter blasphemy to orthodox Muslims. Yet, for Sufis, it is truth. In Hinduism (Paganism), the only reality is God. Everything is Brahma ("God"). This Reality is One, and only "illusion" separates it. The ultimate goal of the Hindu, and Sufi, is to shed these layers of maya like a snake sheds its skins. Once this is done, the individual self or soul merges with the Oversoul ("Brahma"). Of course, the Sufi calls the Oversoul "Allah"; but, a "rose is a rose."

Qaddafi, Khomeini, and the thousands of Muslim terrorists are not "orthodox" or "fundamentalist" Muslims as our liberal media would like us to believe. They are governed by the Sufis. The average orthodox Muslim is law-abiding, peace-loving, and prayerful. He does not believe in his own divinity, like the Sufi. Orthodox Muslims may not be saved, but they believe that Isa (Jesus) will return and reign for a thousand years after he has destroyed the Antichrist.

Orthodox Muslim countries, like Saudi Arabia, and Egypt are friends to the United States and the other Western Powers. They are seeking peaceful ties to Israel. It is the Sufi controlled

Arab states, Libya and Iran, who are our enemies. The
ignorant masses follow the Sufi Imams (leaders) like the
Indian masses follow the gurus: blindly! These Sufi Masters
have pledged to drench the Western world in blood—mostly
ours.

What is their goal? To establish a New World Order, an
"Ottoman Empire" dedicated to the destruction of our Judeo-
Christian society. Who will be the Caliph (prophet, priest, and
king) of this new empire? Will it be Maitreya himself? Let's
see.

## THE MEANING OF MAITREYA

What does Maitreya mean? We saw before that it means
"Merciful One." According to Buddhist prophecies, in the
latter days the Fifth Buddha, Maitreya, shall appear. He shall
be known, as we read earlier, by the fact of his carrying a
waterpot. The symbol of Aquarius (the New Age) is the man
with the waterpot. To understand Maitreya, we must understand Buddhism.

To begin with, Buddhism is nothing more than a sect of
Hinduism. Many Brahmins (Aryans) consider the Buddha
(meaning the "Illuminated One") to be the ninth avatar (reincarnation) of Vishnu. He was born Siddhartha Gautama, a
prince in northern India (near Tibet) about 600 B.C. Brahmin
medicine men told his father that the boy would either be a
great king, or a great teacher. Siddhartha's father was determined that his son would be a king, and not a holy man. So
determined was he, that he shielded Siddhartha from the
Aryan-Luciferian world around him.

One day, Siddhartha got tired of sitting around the palace,
and ventured out for the first time. He saw the terrible suffering of the world around him. He immediately renounced his
princely  titles, and then sought, through meditation and
asceticism, the reason for all the unspeakable suffering he
witnessed. Many years went by, but nothing came.

Finally, while meditating under a tree, Siddartha became
"illuminated." He realized that the horrible suffering was all

part of a plan, and rather than do anything about it, men should simply accept suffering as a necessary part of the Karmic cycle. Siddhartha was unorthodox in one manner only, he suggested that the Brahmins give up their luxurious lifestyles as gods on earth and share in the suffering of the lower castes. A few hundred Brahmins responded, and Gautama's popularity grew. They now called him Buddha.

At first glance, one cannot help but admire him, but there's a catch. At that time (circa 600 B.C.) there was a Renaissance going on. Cyrus the Great, inspired king of Persia, was rebuilding the Temple and Jerusalem for the Jews. Cyrus was a follower of the Persian prophet Zoroaster, who established a religion in direct opposition to the Paganism (Hinduism) that had prevailed for millenia. Christian scholars believe that the wise men mentioned in the New Testament were actually Zoroastrian priests. Their prophet had apparently told them that God himself would descend to earth as King of the Jews. Zoroaster had told his followers to recognize the birth of the Messiah by a new star in the heavens, and to follow that star. The Majai did so, and offered the baby Jesus gold, frankincense, and myrrh (Matt. 2:1-12).

Thousands of Persians who began to enter India found a living hell (the Aryan-Luciferian Society). They began to preach the doctrines of their own prophet Zoroaster, and many of the lower castes began to throw off the heavy yoke and chains of the "God- man" (Brahmins).

Guatama came right in the nick of time! He, with hundreds of other Brahmins, renounced their luxury and suffered with the lower castes. To the lower castes this was a most humbling affair. One might compare it to a slum lord volunteering to live among and help his tenants. The fame of Buddha, and his disciples, travelled far and wide. The lower castes rededicated themselves to the Brahmins, and the proselytization of the Zoroastrians was virtually stopped among the native Hindus.

Soon, however, the Buddha was gone, and his disciples became "God-men" like their fellow Brahmins. The non-

Aryans were once again enslaved. The lower castes believed the lie; they believed the slum-lords had reformed. Yet, it was just a veil to deceive. Once the Zoroastrians were gone, the veils came off; things returned to normal (if you can call a living hell "normal").

Some of the uninitiated Brahmins think Buddha was a heretic for casting himself down to the level of the lower castes. The initiated Brahmins know better. They recognize him as the 9th avatar of Vishnu. How about the 10th? Has he come yet? Not long before the death of the Buddha, one of his main disciples, Ananda, came to him and asked, "Who shall teach us when thou are gone?" The Buddha replied:

> I am not the first Buddha who came upon the earth nor shall I be the last. In due time another Buddha will arise in the world, a holy one, a supremely enlightened one, endowed with wisdom in conduct, auspicious, knowing the universe, an incomparable leader of men, as master of angels and mortals. He will reveal to you the same eternal truths which I have taught you. He will preach his religion, glorious in its origin, glorious at the climax, and glorious at the goal. He will proclaim a religious life, wholly perfect and pure, such as I now proclaim, His disciples will number many thousand, while mine number many hundred.[38]

Then Ananda asked, "How shall we know him?" Then Buddha replied, "He shall be known as Maitreya."[39] The name can mean "Kindness," "Benevolence," "Compassionate," "Loving," "Friendly," or "Merciful." Don't let the name fool you; he will be neither friendly nor merciful to Bible-believing Christians.

## THE MYSTERIOUS MAITREYA

New Age leaders and propagandists accept the vision of renowned psychic Jeane Dixon, as to the birth-date of

Maitreya. On February 5, 1962, Dixon claims to have had a vision of the birth of the New Age "Messiah." In her vision, she claims she saw Pharaoh Ikhnaton and Queen Nefertiti, the patron saints of occultism, with a child in their arms. In the vision the queen held out the infant as an offering to the world. Dixon described the eyes of the child as "all-knowing . . . full of wisdom and knowledge."

As the child grew, there was seen a cross above his head, which grew and grew until it "dripped over the earth in all directions." She says, "Simultaneously, peoples of every race, religion and color, each kneeling and lifting arms in worshipful adoration, surrounded him. They were all as one." Dixon believed this "Messiah" would "bring together all mankind in one all embracing faith . . . the world as we know it will be reshaped and revamped into one without wars or suffering."

Dixon, who claims now to be a dedicated Catholic, has changed her attitude toward this "Child of the East." She wrote that he was to be the Antichrist:

> The circumstances surrounding the birth of the "Child of the East" and the events I have since seen taking place in his life make him appear so Christlike, yet so different, that there is no doubt in my mind that the "child" is the actual person of the Antichrist, the one who will deceive the world in Satan's name.[40]

This was not all. Dixon had decided to turn over even more "state's evidence" against this "Child of the East" that she had, at first, hoped to save the world. She writes that he will become aware of this mission at age twelve (1974). Dixon continues:

> He will then expand his influence, and those around him will finally form a small nucleus of dedicated followers when he reaches the age of nineteen (1981). He will work quietly with them until he is twenty-nine or thirty years old

(1991-92), when the forcefulness and impact
of his presence in the world will begin to bear
his forbidden fruit.

In the same manner as Christ and his disciples
spread the Gospel, so the child and his disciples will propagate the religion of the false
god. The difference will be, however, that they
will not stand alone, but will have the power
and the propaganda machine of the United
States backing them, advancing his cause
beyond anything ever possible.[41]

Who are his disciples, and how shall he rally them? I shall
quote Christian scholar and author Rene Pache. He writes:

That all the nations of Western culture fallen
into apostasy will thus acclaim the Antichrist
would seem to be entirely plausible. But how
can the other peoples be brought unto such a
movement, as, for example, the Moslems who
are so fiercely attached to their faith? But—
strange thing—Moslems themselves look for
a mysterious person, the "hidden Mahdi," who
will bring justice on earth and lead Islam to
triumph while subduing all infidels. Perhaps
the Antichrist will succeed in passing himself
as this awaited Mahdi and in thus rallying
around his very person even the disciples of
Mohammad, not to speak of the followers of
other religions.[42]

Was Dixon correct in her repented second opinion? Was
a child born "in the East" back in 1962 who is now preparing
for world domination? Apparently, Creme hasn't heard about
Dixon's "second opinion" as of yet. In every edition of *Share
International* Creme has a special "Questions and Answers"
section. In the December '85 issue Creme was asked if
Dixon's Messiah was Maitreya. Not knowing that Mrs. Dixon
had since renounced this Messiah as Antichrist, Creme said

he believed that Mrs. Dixon had "Correctly turned into an actual thought form about the return of Christ."

## *TRACKING DOWN MAITREYA*

The above information created distinguishing characteristics that would help me identify Maitreya. Let's look at some of the clues. Creme had stated that his name is a common Moslem one. He stated in the September 1983 issue of *Share International* that Maitreya uses a common "Pakistani" name. This is no contradiction since 98% of Pakistanis are Moslem.

Creme has said elsewhere that his name is as common as "Smith" in England and America. Thus, Creme must be referring to his *last* name. This was easy enough to discover. After a few clues from my connections at Tara Center, and groping through Pakistani telephone directories, I had reason to believe Maitreya's last name was Ahmad. Here are the facts thus far on Maitreya:

- He was born in "the East" in February 1962.

- His last name is Ahmad.

- He is called "Maitreya," but he doesn't go by that name.

- In July 1977, he flew from Karachi, Pakistan, to London, England.

- He is a member and spokesman for an Indo-Pakistani Community in London.

- He occasionally goes to a Moslem mosque, but cannot be considered an "orthodox" Moslem.

&#183; He wears local Moslem dress and, on occasion, Western suits.

&#183; He gives weekly addresses before audiences in Benjali and Urdu (the Pakistani dialects).

&#183; He is tall, thin, with a long nose, long face, and large round eyes.

After the "Day of Declaration" came and went, without Maitreya showing, there was great disappointment among New Agers and journalists. Creme declared that Maitreya didn't show because the media was not willing to link-up to world-wide satellite suggesting that the entire affair was just some sort of money-making scheme or elaborate practical joke. Creme, however, was to get the last laugh.

## *THE IMAM MAHDI LIVES IN LONDON*

While researching the identity of Maitreya, I contacted other investigators. Some of them were Christian authors and researchers. Others were esotericists who didn't agree with Creme. Eventually, through my contacts, I was introduced to a certain young man (who shall be nameless at this point) who seemed to have the leads that I needed.

He told me about a certain article that had appeared in Creme's official periodical, *Share International*. The article was by Benjamin Creme and Peter Liefhebber. The article was entitled "The Imam Mahdi Lives In London." It begins:

> Before Benjamin Creme's announcement in May last year, virtually no-one knew that Maitreya was in London. But a Pakistani journalist has known since 1973 that Maitreya would come to that city. In that year this journalist arrived in London where he has been ever since, awaiting a meeting with Maitreya—the Imam Mahdi. In the light of this

knowledge he has been involved in the search for Maitreya for over a year. *Share International* interviewed him.

The article tells about a certain Pakistani Moslem journalist, but refused to give his name. They wrote:

He asked us not to use his name as he does not seek personal publicity. We were happy to comply with his request. However, we can reveal that he is 37 years old, is on the staff of an Asian daily newspaper produced in London, and that he lost his previous job because he resolutely went on trying to trace the Imam Mahdi.

The unnamed Pakistani journalist told his story to Creme and Liefhebber. He told them that in 1965 he met a man named Fazal Karim, a civil servant in Lahore, Pakistan. Karim told the journalist secret things about his life and family—things he could not have possibly known. The journalist decided that the man was "something special." Over the course of their acquaintance Karim would "materialize all sorts of objects" out of thin air. The journalist was shocked, but continued to see Karim.

Eventually, Karim began to tell him about the coming of the Mahdi—the Promised One of Islam. Karim told him that many of the "orthodox" traditions about the coming of the Mahdi were incorrect. The journalist drifted back and forth from unbelief to thinking that Karim was sent by God. Soon, Karim told him that Mahdi's future location would be in London.

Karim told the journalist that he should go to London because it was there that he would meet the Mahdi. The journalist said that he had no intention of doing it, because he was a friend of President Zia, and had intended to enter politics himself. Karim told him:

You are a worker in the divine kingdom and you must go to London. If you do not you will

be made to go—circumstances will conspire to
lead you there.

The journalist told Karim that he would believe it when it
happened. One week later he lost his job, and became a
political exile. He moved to London and stayed with his older
brother who was already there.

The journalist was not convinced that he was sent by God
to reveal the Mahdi, who lived in London. He tried for over a
year to find him but without success. He was condemned by
fundamentalist Moslems for even suggesting that the Mahdi
would appear in London (fundamentalist Moslems believe he
will appear in Damascus or Jerusalem).

After a year, the journalist gave up. Other journalists
called him "a nut" and had him officially banned from the
BBC Press Club. Attitudes changed, however, when Creme
made the announcements that the World Teacher was in
London. Fellow journalists asked if the journalist had ever
heard of Creme. He told them no, Soon, however, the answer
would change.

When Creme and Liefhebber interviewed the Pakistani
journalist in 1983, he told them about wanting to see Maitreya.
He said, "I do not know when it will happen, but I am certain
that I will eventually see the Mahdi here in London.

The interview ends there, and we never here of this
journalist again in Tara Center publications. Why? Could it
be that the journalist finally got his wish in meeting Maitreya?
Could it be that the sincere journalist discovered that Maitreya
was a man possessed by an evil spirit instead of the Imam
Mahdi?

For an investigative reporter, this journalist would be
relatively easy to find. According to the article, he came from
Pakistan to London in 1974-75. He works for a Pakistani
language newspaper in London—a daily. He was 37 years old
in 1983. He was temporarily banned from the BBC Press
Club.

Certainly, this journalist would be an easy man to find. How many people have been banned from the BBC Press Club because they were turning London inside-out looking for the Imam Mahdi? Let's be serious!

Using my sources, including an individual who actually was in close contact with the leaders of Maitreya's religious community in London, I was able to identify the New Age "Messiah."

Who is Maitreya? He is Kalki, the Destroyer! He comes not to save men's lives but to *destroy* them. He will claim to be the Promised One of all religions. He will claim to be God himself. To prove these claims, he will ostensibly work miracles.

Who is this "Lord" Maitreya now secretly living in London? Let's find out!

# 6.

# PART SIX

## What Is Lord Maitreya's Real Name?

Since 1975 Benjamin Creme has been speaking and writing about the reappearance of the "Christ." He claims to receive his messages telepathically from a "Master"—one of the senior disciples of Maitreya.

At a press conference in Los Angeles on May 14, 1982, Creme informed ninety journalists, representing major news media in the U.S. and Britain, that the Christ had been living in London since July 19,1977 and would come forward if they, acting on behalf of humanity as a whole, would investigate. But, except for coverage of the press conference, the major media took no further action. In the years following, Creme and his coworkers continued to make known Maitreya's presence in the world—helping to create a climate of expectancy. They continued to contact the news media with this information. On July 31,1985, Patricia Pitchon, a free-lance South American journalist living in London, gathered a representative group of twenty-two journalists from countries around the world at a designated meeting place in London. This was the Brick Lane area of London. According to Creme, this "gathering" was accepted by Maitreya, as a symbolic invitation from humanity for him to come forward. Pitchon actually caught a glimpse of Maitreya, whom she described as being tall, wearing white Muslim clothing, having a long nose, and large round eyes.

Since July of 1985, according to Creme, Maitreya has been meeting with and appearing to world leaders, journalists, influential people in every field of endeavor, and to ordinary men and women.

According to Creme, in early April 1988, journalist Patricia Pitchon was summoned to the first of many interviews with a close associate of Maitreya in the Indo Pakistani community of London. During these interviews, the "close associate of Maitreya" (who is never named) relays messages to Pitchon. These messages are mainly predictions of world events. Some of Maitreya's predictions have been the end of the Iran/Iraq war, and the imminent abdication of Mikail Gorbachev as leader of the Soviet Union. New Age propagandist Elizabeth Clare Prophet tells of a "sign" that must be given in order to enter the New Age:

> Don't miss this rare opportunity to experience a dictation from an Ascended Master...by the emerald matrix, the sealing of the servants of God in their foreheads. Be there, and enter the New Age![1]

Other signs have been the phenomenon of cloud formations resembling Christ's image being photographed in different locations from airplanes, strange "crosses of light" appearing in the windows of people around the Tara Center in Los Angeles, and reports from different locations (such as an Israeli village) that the Messiah has appeared unto small groups of people.

The greatest "happening" by far, however, occurred in Nairobi, Kenya, on the 11th of June 1988. In the April 1988 interview between Pitchon and "the Asian Disciple," the journalist was told that, "In three to four week's time Maitreya's mission will begin openly." About three and a half

weeks later something happened. This is a statement from the
Tara Center:

> On June 11, 1988 in Nairobi, Kenya, a remark-
> able stranger appeared at Sister Mary Akatsa's
> faith healing center and addressed the crowd.
> Akatsa introduced him as Jesus Christ. The
> audience was deeply moved, and spontaneous
> healings reportedly occurred. The incident
> received worldwide news coverage. Benjamin
> Creme confirmed from his Master that this
> man was indeed Maitreya—the Christ, in one
> of His many guises, appearing to the people in
> a way in which they would recognize Him.

## MAITREYA HAS APPEARED!

Several news groups recorded the event, including "CNN"
(Cable News Network). How many of the viewers realized
that they were seeing the very face of Maitreya? The "CNN"
crew took a number of close-up camera shots of Maitreya.
This recorded event will be featured in the film entitled *The
New Age Conspiracy.*

The Nairobi, *Kenya Daily,* and *The Kenya Times,* came
out with several large articles on the event. Nyanga wa Muto
and Ben Mitukaa, reporters for *The Kenya Times,* did an article
that was featured only a week after the event. They entitled
their article, "Did Jesus Visit Kawangware?" (June 26, 1988).
Their article included a photograph of "A mysterious light that
shocked worshippers at Akatsa's place a week before the
'Jesus miracle' occurred." Kawangware is a Muslim village
within the city limits of Nairobi. The light from heaven was
not to be the only strange event.

Mr. Job Mutungi, a reporter for *The Kenya Times,* did a
large article on what happened on the 11th of June. Mutungi
was right there at Akatsa's center when the event occurred.
He writes:

> About 6,000 worshippers at the Muslim Vil-
> lage, Kawangware, Nairobi, believe they saw

Jesus Christ, in broad daylight last week. It may be hard to believe, but nothing will move them, because "Jesus" addressed them and assured them of a comeback, very soon.

The scene was at the Church of Bethlehem,where Mary Sinaida Akatsa, conducts miracle prayers, praying for the sick, the blind, cripples, mad people, the barren and others facing all sorts of personal problems.

On Saturday June 4, 1988, a big, bright star was sighted above the skies by worshippers. It was unusually brighter than ordinary stars. The time was 1pm. But on Saturday June 11, it was different. Worshippers were busy singing Mungu ni Mwema, a popular Swahili hymn, when Mary Akatsa interjected. She announced that God had spoken to her and told her to "await a miracle because a very important guest would be coming to give her a very vital message . . ." People braced themselves for the unknown while others stared blankly at her, their mouths agape with awe and bewilderment. Five minutes later, she asked those who were singing to stop, as the long awaited message had arrived. "Jesus! Jesus! Jesus of Nazareth!," went the loud whispers from the crowd as they raised up their hands in submission and divine welcome. The tall figure of a bare footed white robed and bearded man, appeared from nowhere and stood in the middle of the crowd.

From the two articles mentioned, we can reconstruct what happened. Mary Senaida Akatsa is a renowned faith healer in Kenya. She works mostly among the poor Muslims of Nairobi. Her mother died when she was seven months pregnant with Mary, but the child was saved by an emergency post-mortem caesarian section.

Early in life, Mary had a strange vision. She heard the voice of her grandmother, who was dead. Mary followed the voice and saw in front of her "a calm merciful looking man in a pure white cloth"—standing. She later said that the man was Jesus, and that he had given her special powers. She became well known for her healings and cures. Mary started a large healing center at The Church of Bethlehem in Kawangware, Nairobi, Kenya. On June 4, 1988, a bright star appeared above the Church of Bethlehem compound in broad daylight. A Reverend Bonnke went on national television and radio declaring that Jesus would soon appear at the church compound. Also, on that day, a photograph was taken of a mysterious light that descended and fell upon the crowd at the healing center.

One week later, a tall bearded white-robed man appeared outside the residence of a Mr. Gurnam Singh, a member of the Church of Bethlehem. The white-robed man was praying in the Muslim fashion, but when Singh came out to ask the man what he was doing on his property, the man asked Singh if he could be taken to the church compound. Mr. Singh agreed.

Once at the compound the mysterious white-robed man appeared before the crowd and walked to Mary's side. The man addressed the crowd in pure Swahili, with no trace of an accent. He told the crowd that all nations were to be one, with Christ at the head. He promised them to be faithful, and that he would return.

The white-robed man left the meeting with Mr. Singh. Once they reached a distance from the compound, Mr. Singh and others reported that the man asked for the car to halt. When the car was stopped, the man got out and walked to the side of the road where he "vanished into thin air."

About the most reliable witness to the events was one Tobias Onyango, a Nairobi lawyer. He said that he didn't witness any healings, but did witness the bright star in daylight. How should we view the events in Nairobi? Creme has declared that this was indeed Maitreya. Someone even notified "CNN" of the event ahead of time. They televised the occurrence the following day over "CNN" stations.

A few questions come to mind. Why such an obscure place as Kenya to make the initial appearance? Why to poor Muslims coming to be healed at a Christian church? What significance do these things hold.

The answers soon became clear. To occultists (esotericists), evolution created man and is responsible for his progress toward becoming God. Evolutionists claim that Kenya is the first home of mankind. The star in midday that appeared over the Church of Bethlehem is a satanic twist on the star that appeared over the town of Bethlehem when the one true Christ was born. The one in whom Maitreya came to was Mary Akatsa. He appeared in her center at the Church of Bethlehem compound. Jesus came through the womb of Mary, the betrothed of Joseph. Why to Muslims? Remember, Maitreya must convince the Muslim world that he is their Imam Mahdi. Those that helped Maitreya in his visit were the pastors (shepherds) of the Church of Bethlehem. Those that brought the good news of the Messiah were lowly shepherds from Bethlehem. This is just the beginning. Benjamin Creme commented on the article by Job Mutungl:

> Maitreya's appearance was in keeping with the crowd's expectations as Jesus Christ, hence his bearded face and biblical robes. The "bucketful of blessings" with which Maitreya promises to return is an allusion to Himself as the "Water Carrier," symbol of the Aquarian Age. The correct translation of the Swahili word used by Maitreya is "pitcher," not "bucket." The "strange sporadic light" emanating from Maitreya's head and feet described by Job Mutungi are also habitually seen by those around Maitreya now.

## MAITREYA'S ASIAN DISCIPLE

According to the Tara Center, Maitreya has now appeared openly and will make many more open appearances before the "Day of Declaration" occurs. On the Day of Declaration we shall known his name, and other particulars but for now his true identity is a secret. Not anymore.

Journalist Patricia Pitchon receives messages from Maitreya on a monthly basis, via Maitreya's Asian Disciple in London. Maitreya's messages through Creme were, at best, obscure. Now they are getting very direct and even prophetic.

Through my contacts within the New Age movement, and even those dealing with the community Maitreya belongs to, I have discovered the identity of Maitreya's mysterious "Asian Disciple." His name is Maulana Ata ul Mujeeb Rashed. He is the Imam of the London Mosque of the Ahmadiyyah movement in Islam. He is also "missionary in-charge" for the Ahmadiyyah Muslim movement in the United Kingdom.

The Ahmadiyyah movement in Islam is by far the largest and most powerful of the international Sufi movements. There are perhaps over fourteen thousand Ahmadis (as they are called) in Great Britain alone. Worldwide, there are between ten and fifteen million in every Muslim nation, and even in large numbers in Europe and the United States.

## THE AHMADIYYAH MOVEMENT

Before we can reveal the identity of Maitreya, we need to understand more about the religious community in which he reportedly belongs. Occultists know that 1890 was an eventful year. In that year the king of the world came above ground for a special appearance. He appeared to a Buddhist temple in Narabanchi, Outer Mongolia (in the Gobi Desert). A monk named Hutuktu recounted the event to a Russian occultist by the name of Ferdin and Ossendowski, who relates it here for us:

Do you see this throne? One night in winter,
several horsemen rode into the
monastery....Then one of the strangers
mounted the throne, where he took off his
bashly or caplike head covering. All the Lamas
fell to their knees as they recognized the man
who had been long ago described in the sacred
bulls of Dalai Lama,Tashi Lama and Bogdo
Khan. He was the man to whom the whole
world belongs and who has penetrated into all
the mysteries of Nature. He pronounced a short
Tibetan prayer, blessed all his hearers and
afterwards made predictions for the coming
half century. This was thirty years ago and in
the interim all his prophecies are being
fulfilled. During his prayers before that small
shrine in the next room this door opened of its
own accord, the candles and lights before the
altar lighted themselves and the sacred braziers
without coals gave forth great streams of
incense that filled the room. And then, without
warning, the king of the world and his
companions disappeared from among us.
Behind him remained no trace save the folds
in the silken throne coverings which smoothed
themselves out and left the throne as though
no one had sat upon it.[2]

Our attention must now turn to India. In 1890 there came
a Muslim man in India who claimed to be the Promised One
of all Religions. His name was Ghulam Ahmad. One of his
descendants writes about him:

The Ahmadiyyah movement is not an old
movement; it is only about thirty-four years
old (1924). The movement was founded by
Hazrat [Reverend] Mirza Sir Ghulam Ahmad
(on whom be peace) under an express divine
command. He claimed to be the Mahdi, whose

advent had been foretold by the Holy Prophet
Muhammad (on whom be peace and the
blessings of God) and the Messiah, whose
advent had been foretold in the Bible and in
certain Islamic books . . .

Ghulam wrote many books, and organized his Sufi
movement that extended all over the world. There are
Ahmadi mosques in every country of the world influencing
and coordinating with the occult groups. The first Ahmadi
"mission" to the West was started in London, England.

Ghulam Ahmad finally died in May of 1908 and was
succeeded by his son. Every successor has since been called
the Khalifah-ul-Masih (Successor of the Messiah). The
Reader may now be asking, "How can Ghulam Ahmad be
Maitreya, since he has been dead since 1908?" The answer to
this is simple. Each Khalifah ("Successor") of Ghulam was
to carry his "spirit and power." It should be interesting to note
that Ghulam Ahmad died in the Spring of 1908. In the fall
of that same year, Maitreya entered into and possessed the
body of Krishnamurti. We know, of course, that this possession failed. Yet, the evil spirit (entity) that possessed Ghulam
and Krishnamurti is possessing the man called "Maitreya"
right now. This time the Masters hope for success. Who is
the individual now possessed?

Benjamin Creme declares that Maitreya is now in a human
body, and is a spokesman for a group or community in a
well-known modern country. Creme later identified the
modern country as England. Creme later revealed that
Maitreya lives and works among an Indo-Pakistani
community in London. Which community? The Ahmadiyya
movement always refers to itself as the "Community."

Some journalists have hunted for Maitreya among the
Hindus of London or the "orthodox" Muslims there. Pakistanis are Muslim, and Hindus are Indians. Rarely would they
join together in a social atmosphere, even if they did live in
the same villages or cities. It is unlikely that they would choose

one individual to be their combined spokesman. The Pakistanis would demand a Muslim, and the Indians would demand a Hindu.

This dilemma is solved only if the "Indo-Pakistani community" in London turns out to be the London Ahmadi Community. Ghulam placed his headquarters in Qadian, India. In the late 1940s, British India was split into India, and East and West Pakistan. Those Muslims in the new India were exiled to one of the two Pakistans, and those Hindus in either Pakistan were exiled to India.

Though Qadian fell just within the Indian border, the Indian government considered the movement Muslim. They were forced to move their headquarters to Rabwah, West Pakistan. However, because of their close affinity with Hinduism, many Ahmadis were allowed to live and work in India. West Pakistan eventually became Pakistan, and East Pakistan became Bangladesh. Ghulam ordered his followers to create a mission to the West, headquartered in London, England— the seat of the empire that ruled India.

Creme tells us that the "Christ" flew by jet from Karachi, Pakistan, to London, England, in July of 1977, and that he has been giving hundreds of presentations since that time. The Ahmadi missionary was giving similar presentations back in the late 1950s. Who was he? He was Mubarak Ahmad. It seems that each descendant of Ghulam, before he becomes the new Khalif, is assigned to the London Mission as Missionary-in-Charge, or, if you will, chief spokesman for the Ahmaddiyyah Community. Maitreya is the man. Who is he?

The man proclaimed by Benjamin Creme and revered by millions of Easterners is a man still in his twenties, now living in London. Only Creme, Ahmadi leaders, and certain New Age leaders know that this man is their "Christ"—the "Lord" Maitreya who will unify and lead first the New Age, and then the world. This man is destined to become the Khalifat-ul-

Masih V leader of the fourteen million Ahmadis. He is the great, great-grandson of Ghulam Ahmad.

In July of 1977 he was commissioned by his uncle, the Khalifat-ul-Masih IV, to take control of the London Mission of the Ahmadiyya Community. In that month he flew from the airport to Karachi, Pakistan, to London, England. He was expected to further his own education, and to learn from his elders for a number of years before actually taking control of the mission.

According to a prophecy, Ghulam would appear in London, England, giving speeches in English not in his person, but through one of his successors (Khalifas). In the last chapter we discussed how the Christians of the Middle-Ages considered the Turks to be devils incarnate. Ruling over the Ottoman (Turkish) Empire was the Caliph (a variant spelling of Khalif). The Caliphs were the prophets, priests, and kings of Islam, or, we should say, Sufism. Orthodox Islam do not have Caliphs. Orthodox Muslims adhere to the Quran only—a work based on the Old and New Testaments, apocryphal material, and Muhammad's personal revelations. The Ahmadis are the only ones claiming to have Caliphs. Kaddafi and Khomeini have been promising their peoples that the Imam Mahdi will soon appear, and that he will become the Caliph of a new Muslim Empire. There are now almost a billion Muslims in the world, and Sufism is gathering three million of them each year. For what?

It may be just a coincidence that in the Koine Greek, the language of the Apocalyse, the word "Caliph" (or Khalif), takes on new meanings. Robert F. Riggs, an occultist and an accomplished student of Islam, wrote a commentary on the book of Revelation. Here Riggs comments on the subject of the "mark of the beast":

> Countless attempts have been made to assign
> the number 666 to   favored villains over the
> past nineteen centuries. One early attempt was
> to give the number to "Nero Caesar," but the

literal value of his name is only 616, fifty short
of the required value. Other attempts have
been made to equate 666 to the geometrical
value of the names of the Pope, Luther,
Napoleon, the Kaiser, and Hitler. Most of these
attempted solutions are too contrived to be
considered seriously, since they employ such
strategies as incorrect spelling, abbreviations,
and obscure notation. About the best that can
be hoped for is to derive a spelling of "The
Caliph" that is recognizable to a modern Greek
who is literate in Koine. Both    (The) Callef
and Cal'lif  meet this requirement. Both spell-
ings also produce the value 666.[3]

The first man to assume the title of Caliph was
Mu'awaiyah, a Sufi. He and his descendants ruled Islam
during the Ottoman Empire era. The last of his descendants
died about six hundred years ago. The family name was the
Umayyid. They originated in Damascus, Syria. Riggs continues by saying, "Since Mu'awaiyah committed an act of
blasphemy by assuming the title of Caliph, it should not be
surprising if his assumed title The Caliph has the value 666."[4]
It is also not surprising that Creme hints of Maitreya's affinity
with the ancient Caliphs. Creme writes: "In his next incarnation, as Apollonius of Tyana, Jesus became a Master. He lives
now in a Syrian body which is some 600 years old...."[5]  The
last Umayyad Caliph was assassinated in 1358, and he was,
of course, a Syrian. After that the Sufis went underground.
Now they have reemerged.

The eldest male child in the direct line of Ghulam has
always been designated the Khalifat-ul-Masih. The first
Khalifa was called Nuruddin, the son of Ghulam. He became
the Khalifat-ul-Masih I (the First Successor of the Messiah).
Next was his eldest son, Mamood Ahmad. Mahmood wrote
of himself:

I am not the khalifa of only the Qadianis nor
only of India. I am not the caliph of the

promised Messiah. So I am the caliph for
Afghanistan, the Arab world, Iran, China,
Japan, Europe, America, Africa, Sumatra,
Java: so far so that I am caliph for Britain also
and my sultanate extends over all the con-
tinents of the world.

Of course, that was just wishful thinking. However, could
it be a prophecy regarding not him individually, but the
Ahmadi Khalifate? The Ahmadi Khaifas have always had a
double-standard, like their Aryan brothers. Eshad Azheer
quotes a certain witness to a trial involving the second Khaifa:

Mahmood Ahmad had a young maid servant.
She once went to the   dispensary of Ihsan Ali
Qadiyani, to buy some medicines. Ihsan Ali
deceived her and took her to an empty room
behind the drugstore and raped her. When this
maid, named Salma, returned to the house, she
informed the Qadiani khalifa of what had happened. The khalifa called Ihsan Ali and asked
Salma to beat him with a shoe ten times which
she did. Then he let  Ihsan Ali alone and he
want away.

The acts of the Ahmadi Khalifas did nothing but outrage
the puritanical orthodox Muslims. In a visit to Paris, the
Khalifat-ul-Masih II was seen visiting a theatre that featured
nude dancers. Questioned by the Muslim press when he got
back to Pakistan, Mahmood Ahmad declared, "I visited it only
to see the evils of Western civilization."

Every Khalifa was to bear the spirit and power of Ghulam.
The first Khalifa, Nuruddin Ahmad, declared:   "I swear by
the Mighty Allah that it is He who has made me His
Viceregent. So whoever wishes to snatch from me the mantle
of this viceregency, he may. God, His wisdom and His Will,
wish to make me your leader and your caliph. Say then
whatever you want. All that you impute to me and insult me

with does not reach me but returns to God as He it is who has made me the caliph."

## *THE DIVINE LIGHT*

The Khalifas ruled the Ahmadis with an iron fist. They spread Sufism from secret societies into every part of the globe. There are now around fourteen million Ahmadis proper. Take that number with the tens of thousands of Sufi masters that rule in every Arab state, Russia, China, etc. Yet, none of these Khalifas were to be like the last Khalifa. He is called the "Divine Light." Ghulam says in a revelation that he received regarding this ultimate Caliph that "He shall be of thy own seed and of thine own progeny and race. His name is Emanuel and also Bashir. He is given the Holy Spirit. He is free from sin."

The "Divine Light" was to be a descendant of Ghulam Ahmad—of his seed. He is given all sorts of messianic titles and abilities. He is, like the vision by psychic Jeane Dixon, going to be born on a Monday, and his influence will extend over the four corners of the earth. Could this "finally appointed Mahdi" be Maitreya? Could he be the one who shall take the reins of government: first over the Muslim world, with its uncountable legions and bottomless wealth through oil, and then the rest of the world? The "world" would never let an orthodox Muslim take charge. Orthodox Muslims have an ethical code which would frighten a Puritan. However, if a leader came along claiming to be the "Promised One" of all religions, and no religion, then he might be accepted. He would be accepted if he taught a morality, or shall I say immorality, that appealed to the natural man.

He would tell the world that Jesus is dead, and that they were all gods. The nations would lift themselves up in their sins before God. What little resemblance of humility they have left will be gone. The world dictator will promise the nations that they can be one in peace and wealth. If only those fanatical Christians were out of the way.

## *MAITREYA IDENTIFIED*

Now we have come to the identity of Maitreya. According to Ghulams revelation, the "Divine Light" will appear with Fazl. Could this "Fazl" be the same person as Fazil Karim the Sufi master? The Ahmadi Khalfas are as follows:

1) Hazrat Moulvi Nur ud Din (Khalfat-ul-Masih I)

2) Hazrat Mirza Bashir ud Din Mahmood Ahmad (Khalifat-ul-Masih II)

3) Hazrat Mirza Nasir Ahmad (Khalifat-ul-Masih III)

4) Hazrat Mirza Tahir Ahmad (Khalifat-ul-Masih IV) Tahir Ahmad is the present Head of the Ahmadiyyah movement who became so in June of 1982. It was supposed to be June of '82 that Maitreya would make his announcement.

Who is Maitreya? Let's see what we have now. We know that he goes by a common Muslim name. We know that he dresses in Pakistani clothes, and speaks Pakistani dialects. We know that he is from Pakistan. He is a spokesman for an Indo-Pakistani community in London. From my research, we know that this community is the London Ahmadi Community. We know that he is a descendant of Ghulam Ahmad. We know that he is the "Divine Light," the ultimate Mahdi who will bear the spirit and power of Ghulam. Since he bears Ghulam's "power and spirit," he also inherits the titles of Ghulam. Ahmad, as you remember, claimed to be the Promised One of all religions, including the "Lord" Maitreya. Being the promised Caliph would also mean this individual would inherit the title of Maitreya.

Who is he? According to my sources inside the Ahmadiyyah community in London, he is a young man (born in

February 1962) by the name of Rahmat Ahmad. He is a direct descendant of Ghulam Ahmad. He came from Karachi, Pakistan by plane to London in July of 1977. His photograph is in the back of this book.

Since the present head of the Ahmadiyyah Movement has no sons (he has four daughters), Rahmat Ahmad is next in line for the Khalifate. Only his closest disciples know his true identity as the last of the Caliphs.

The name Rahmat has certain interesting meanings. In 1936 a Sufi master in India, U. Ali, wrote a book entitled *Mohammed In Ancient Scriptures*. In his book he talked much about the coming of Maitreya, and he commented on the Arabic equivalent to that name: "Rahmat is the arabic equivalent of Maitreya. Benevolence, loving kindness, friendliness, compassion, mercy or mercifulness, all words of similar import are all expressed by the Arabic word Rahmat." That's not all. The name Rahmat has other occult meanings as well. According to Donald A. Mackenzie, in his *Egyptian Myth and Legend*, the Egyptian god Ra is the lord of the air and the god of Mendes.

Is it a coincidence that Paul calls Satan the "prince of the power of the air" in Ephesians 2:2? In Hebrew, the term for "prince" is Sar, which can mean either captain or chief. Mendes refers to the sacred caverns of Egypt. Occultists throughout the centuries have worshipped the "Goat of Mendes." Naturally, the goat is one of the biblical symbols for Lucifer. Ra is just another name for Lucifer. Egyptian paintings depict Ra carrying in one hand a sickle, and in the other a hammer. These just happen to be the Communist symbols.

It will become clear later how the unification of East and West will facilitate Maitreya in gaining control of all New Age religions. Maat was seen as Mother Nature, or Mother Earth. Another name for her was Isis. In India she was known as Kali. In Palestine she was known as Ashteroth. Her, and Baal

(Satan) were worshipped with the Baalim ("Masters"). Their chief enemy was Jehovah.

The RA-MAAT represents, in occultism, the Yin-Yang, the combined Force of light and darkness. To occultists this Force is impersonal and can be used for either good or evil. Swami Vivekananda, a Hindu guru and High Initiate, talks about "god" as being both good and evil: "Who can say that God does not manifest Himself as Evil as well as Good? But only the Hindu dares to worship him in the evil...How few have dared to worship death, or Kali. Let us worship death."[6] Who is this strange god anyway? A god in whom is good and evil, light and dark. Simply put, he doesn't exist. However, the Bible informs us that "Satan himself is transformed into an angel of light" (2 Cor. 11:14).

Lucifer is all evil, all dark; but in order to deceive the uninitiated, he will appear as an angel of light. Once he has initiated them, the veil comes off, and his true, one and only, evil nature is revealed. Many New Agers—the uninitiated variety—claim that they came to the New Age by a vision or dream of an angel of light. By the time this angel shows his true colors—all black—it is often too late. The New Agers are often unable to break away. Impossible? Look at drug addicts and alcoholics. They are bound. The New Ager begins to experience psychic visions and healings, but, when the visions become nightmares and the healings become unhealthy, he or she is often trapped.

*This is Lord Maitreya (Rahmat Ahmad). On June 11, 1988 in Nairobi, Kenya, he appeared at the Faith Healing Center of Sister Mary Akatsa. Sister Akatsa introduced him as Jesus Christ. "CNN" news crew took a number of close-up camera shots. (Photograph courtesy of Share International, Amsterdam, Holland).*

When the present Khalifat-ul-Masih dies Rahmat Ahmad will become the Khalifat-ul-Masih V. He will then control not only the Ahmadis, but the Sufi networks. Soon, he will be able to control all the New Age movement. We will see later that the New Age movement is striving to control the nations already. Back in June of 1982 Tahir Ahmad was ailing, and it was thought among the Ahmadis that his eldest nephew, Rahmat, would become the new head of the movement. This was not to be. Tahir Ahmad is the head, but he is old and ailing again. The time for Rahmat's Day of Declaration may be soon.

Why did Rahmat Ahmad choose Kenya for his initial appearance? Because, again, evolutionists claim it is the birthplace of man. Kenya has had an Ahmadi Mission since 1961. According to Mubarak Ahmad, a relative of Rahmat and a chief Ahmadi propagandist, "The headquarters of the Kenya Mission is in Nairobi at the Ahmadiyya mosque—an imposing structure built by the community in 1931.

Ghulam Ahmad taught Spiritualism, reincarnation, karma, and used narcotics. He prophesied the deaths of hundreds of people, and most of them died either by a knife in the back or poison in the stomach. He claimed that Jesus was dead and buried in India and that a special ointment cured Jesus on the cross. Yet, this ointment could not save Ghulam from cholera—which he died of in 1908. He declared that descendant of his, the last Khalifa, would carry his spirit and power—Mahdi, Maitreya, and Promised Messiah of all religions. Rahmat Ahmad is destined to become the fifth Caliph. Will he claim to be the last?

The man who is Maitreya is already possessed by the evil spirit from the pit (Shamballah). He will be able to work miracles and, through his lying flatteries, deceive the nations into accepting him as their "Lord." Of course, not all will accept him. Evangelical and fundamentalist Christians will refuse to accept him. What shall be our fate? How will Maitreya take power? When shall all this happen?

A New Ager may now be saying, "So what. Don't you believe in freedom of religion? Can't we believe in our own Christ and you believe in yours?" The fact is that their "Christ" will not allow me freedom to worship my Savior. He will first astonish the world with his superhuman intelligence, and he will flatter the world with his lies. However, once in power, he will demand to be worshipped as God. His establishment of a New World Religion and a New World Order will not prevent World War Three; it will guarantee it! Why? Because, by his Hindu name, he is Kalki, The Destroyer.

Benjamin Creme's ad says that Maitreya "has not as yet declared His true station, and His location is known to only a very few disciples . . . soon the Christ will acknowledge His identity . . . From that time, with His help, we will build a new world." According to the Aryans, Kalki must destroy this old world first and then create a new one. P. Thomas writes, "For this purpose, it is fabled, Vishnu will appear in the world as Kalki riding on a charger, waving the sword of destruction in his right hand."[7] The Great Invocation, chanted by perhaps half a billion New Agers, in calling forth Maitreya, pleads, "Let the Rider from the Secret Place come forth." They know not what they do.

The uninitiated New Agers believe that they are helping to bring a new age of peace, prosperity, and happiness to the earth. They can't be bothered with such "ignorant" concepts as repenting of sins. They are their own gods. Initiated New Agers believe that the entire world will be completely destroyed by Kalki, but that they will sit in palaces of light in Shamballah awaiting the next world and future incarnations as gods.

The Christians know the truth. Shamballah is Hell, and the palaces of light will prove a bit too hot for the initiated. The uninitiated will either become initiated, or be quickly destroyed. Christians know that if they suffer and die, Jesus will greet them on the other side. Maitreya comes to destroy the world not for a better one, but because his master hates God and his creation. How different is this "Christ" from the

True One, who said, For the Son of Man is not come to destroy men's lives, but to save them.

Christians recognize and worship Jesus as the one and only incarnation of God. He is the second person of the Godhead who came down to dwell with men in the flesh and to give his life as a propitiation for our sins. Luciferians believe in reincarnation, and that Vishnu, the second person of the unholy godhead, has reincarnated himself into ten different bodies. We still have the records of the 8th reincarnation (Krishna) and the 9th reincarnation (Buddha) of Vishnu. Of course, these aren't reincarnations at all, but repossessions of an evil spirit into the bodies of human beings. The avatars told of others before and after them who would teach their disciples. Jesus made it clear that he, and he alone, was the only way to life and salvation.

In the next chapter, we will examine the teachings of Maitreya. We will take a closer look at the plans for the New World Order, and how Maitreya plans to convince the world to leave Jesus, and worship himself. We shall also see what plans are now in store for those Christians who refuse to worship the New Age "Messiah."

# 7.

# PART SEVEN

## The Teachings Of Maitreya (Rahmat Ahmad)

The Christian Faith is very simple. It begins like this, "For God so loved the world." The inevitable result of that love is unique.

> He gave his only begotten Son, that whosoever believeth in him should not perish, but have everlasting life. For God sent not his Son unto the world to condemn the world; but that the world through him might be saved. (John 3:16-17)

Saved from what? Our enemies, of course! Who are our enemies? Death and sin. Can the mystery of the Cross be explained? We know that when we abuse our physical bodies we run a debt that can only be paid back with sacrifice. We must exercise, which means physical discomfort and pain. If we do not exercise, then we pay the debt in a different way; we then shall suffer pain and disease. Physicians understand this system of debt and payment very well when it comes to the body. This carries over to every aspect of life. If a farmer abuses his land, he runs a debt of scarred and barren land, and he must pay. Agriculturalists understand this system of debt and repayment very well when it comes to the earth.

In the old days, miners would work sixteen hours a day, seven days a week in the dirty, and dark bowels of the earth. The mining companies would keep the miners' pay low, and their expenses high; so workers' debt would always be greater than their earnings. An old saying of miners was, "I owe my soul to the company store." The miners were slaves, locked in forever to the mine companies. If the miners tried to move, or refused to work, the mine owners put them into prison.

Because of sin we come under the dominion of Satan, and he wishes to keep our wages low and our expenses high so that we might be slaves to him. This is how he takes control of lives and will eventually force the world to worship him. He enslaved mankind to our enemies. Who are our enemies? Death and sin. So too, the Masters of Wisdom promise wisdom, to make us wise, but their paycheck to you is captivity. Jesus came to set the prisoners free by the Cross. Lucifer wants you to suffer eternally in the halls of Shamballah (Hell), but Jesus wants to set you free from eternal suffering and torment, and lead you back to Paradise where he will wipe your tears away forever.

How can he set us free from the chains of Kali (Death) and the fetters of Hell (Shamballah)? By his atonement, which is symbolized by his Cross. Though Lucifer wants us forever in debt, Jesus offers to set us free of it. What are his terms? Follow him. The foundation of Christianity is his suffering and death in payment of our spiritual debt.

Christian author Texe Marrs tells about the New Age teaching that Jesus never died on the Cross: "Peter Lemesurier, an occult pyramidologist and prolific New Age writer, has an even more blatant account of Jesus' death. He suggests that Jesus was a member of the Essene sect, a radical Jewish group that sought to overthrow the Romans and the throning of Jesus as king. Lemesurier proposes that the

Essenes snatched Jesus off the cross before He physically died . . ." and this is why the tomb was empty.[1]

This "theory" accepted by New Agers is not new, Ghulam Ahmad first penned it about one hundred years ago. Liberal New Testament scholar Hugh Schoenfeld shocked the world several decades ago when he came out with his international best-seller *The Passover Plot*. According to this plot, Jesus was never supposed to die on the Cross. He was given a special drug to simulate death.

Even if Jesus was given some mysterious drug to simulate death, he would have needed months, not a matter of hours, to recover from the terrible flogging and other tortures he had received. And the Bible tells us specifically that he died (Luke 23:46) on the Cross.

If New Age leaders and propagandists believe that Jesus survived the Cross, then what do they believe he did after that? They preach that he went to India and became a guru. Their evidence? Once again, they don't tell us. New Age leader, Elizabeth Clare Prophet, describes this guru Jesus in India in her book *The Lost Years of Jesus*. Edgar Cayce, the occult "sleeping prophet" whom New Agers love to read, also tells of Jesus in India.

When I first read Ms. Prophet's book I was amazed to find that she actually had a map of Jesus' route from the Holy Land to India and Tibet. I traced the route—through Persia, Pakistan, to Banares, up to Leh, and back to Srinagar. Then it hit me! This was the route Apollonius of Tyana took in his Eastern journeys. Could this be a coincidence?

Now we have come full circle. It has been the plan of the Masters, and Sanat Kumara himself, to replace Jesus with Apollonius in the minds of men. In other words, Satan and his demonic hosts have been planning to substitute the true Christ (Jesus) with their Antichrist (Apollonius). How can they do this? Let's take a look at Creme's answer. We must remember that Creme is an occultist. To esotericists there are different levels of reality and truth. Deception is seen as a tool to protect higher truths. Let's "translate" Creme's answer.

Creme said that Jesus quickly came into incarnation again as Apollonius of Tyana. What did Creme mean? He means that the concept of Christ Consciousness that the world has recognized in Jesus, has now been transferred to Apollonius. In other words, Jesus is no longer the Christ, now the Christ is Apollonius.

Creme admits that it was Apollonius, and not Jesus, that lived, worked, and was buried in Kashmir; and that the legends and books telling about this actually refer to Apollonius. Apollonius is now in "the place of" Jesus as the Messiah. Creme says that Apollonius "has had two more physical bodies since" he was known as the philosopher from Tyana. This means that Apollonius, or the evil spirit that possessed the man Apollonius, has possessed two other individuals since Apollonius. Could this mean Ghulam Ahmad and Krishnamurti?

Creme declares that Apollonius is now "in a Syrian body some 640 years of age." Well, people just don't live that long. We must remember that Creme is speaking esoterically. What does he mean? The last of the Umayyid Caliphs, a Syrian, died about 640 years ago. The Umayyid Caliphs were pompous, proud, terrible, and merciless toward Christians. They dedicated their lives and empires to the destruction of Christianity.

### How Is The Initiation Accomplished?

It goes like this:

1) New Agers are told that all religions are one, and that Jesus was a great Master.

2) They are told that evidence proves that Jesus, during his eighteen "lost years," became a guru in India.

3) They are then told that Jesus never died on the Cross, but lived and returned to India—dying and being buried in Kashmir.

4) They are then told that the Bible cannot be trusted. How could it? For it teaches that Jesus died on the Cross, etc., things the New Ager now prides himself on knowing wasn't true.

5) They are then told that they are initiated, and that Jesus did die, but was quickly reincarnated as Apollonius of Tyana. Apollonius was the true Christ, and it is he that is buried in Kashmir. Since it is Jesus' "consciousness" that was reborn in Apollonius, New Agers don't feel that they were lied to. They feel snug in the fact that they now understand these "higher truths."

6) They are then told that Apollonius has had two more bodies, but is now (the third body) inhabiting a six hundred year old Syrian body. Those are the six degrees of initiation. How can any rational being believe such obvious lies? The answer is simple. Muslims don't read the New Testament, and, even if they did, they would more likely believe a Muslim (like the Ahmadis claim to be) over a Christian. New Agers don't read the Bible. When they are shown that the Bible refutes New Age teachings, they usually say that the Bible has been changed from what it was originally. Their evidence? The channeled entities that speak through mediums.

The Ahmadis have not stopped in their effort to "Break the Cross." In June, 1978, the Ahhmadiyyah Community of Great Britain sponsored a three-day "international conference" on the subject. They invited scholars from all over the globe. The conference was called, "The Deliverance Of Jesus From The Cross." Catholic Cardinal Hume, of Britain, sent two representatives. Many of the Bishops of the Anglican church "sent greetings of goodwill and said they would be praying for it." This is all part of the unification taking place even now in the 90s that will result in an ultimate synthesis of East and West.

When Maitreya appears, he shall talk with great wisdom. He shall cry Peace! He'll talk about the nations becoming one, the end of hunger, war, and injustice for all. The leaders of the world will claim that he is indeed the one to rule. The masses will see him as their Promised One. Instead of peace he will bring war, and instead of prosperity, there will be terrible suffering.

Maitreya will declare that "negative karmic forces" are to blame. What are these forces? The fundamentalist Christians who refuse to worship him. They will be blamed for everything bad. They will refuse his mark. Then, what has been planned for centuries will happen—the final solution to the "Christian" problem.

Occultists believe in and worship nature. Nature is personified in their minds by the Mother Goddess: be her name Kali, Tara, Gaia, or whatever. High Initiates believe that they must sacrifice to her to keep her content—human sacrifice. The Maharishi Mahesh Yogi, the head of Transcendental Meditation, has declared the fate of the "unfit" of the world. He says there are not and "will not be a place for the unfit. The fit will lead, and if the unfit are not coming along there is no place for them . . . In the Age of Enlightenment there is not place for ignorant people. Nature will not allow ignorance to prevail. It just can't. Nonexistence of the unfit has been the law of nature."[2]

New Age propagandist Ruth Montgomery, called the "Herald of the New Age," has declared that in the New Age "Millions will survive and millions won't. Those who won't will go into the spirit state." Montgomery says not to worry, that all this is just "a cleansing process of Mother Earth."[3] Montgomery states that mankind, in the New Age, will go through a quantum leap of evolution. However, there will be those that try to hinder such progress; those who are to blame for making this world such a mess that it's in now. "The souls who helped to bring on the chaos of the present century will have passed into spirit to rethink their attitudes . . ."[4]

The "Herald" of the New Age assures us that "Millions will survive and millions won't. Those that won't will go into the spirit state, because there truly is no death." This was the lie of Lucifer in the Garden of Eden. He said, "Ye shall not surely die" (i.e., "there is no death"). Once in the spirit realm these "ignorant" and "unfit" souls will have a chance to learn to change their consciousness, since the living New Agers will be able to "communicate with those in spirit . . .beyond the grave."[5]

Another chief New Age propagandist, a Dr. Christopher Hyatt, wrote an article entitled "The Christian Fundamentalist Problem." He said that the fundamentalist Christians were the Guards of the Old Age, and that the New Age meant a changing of the guards. Sounds peaceful enough, but wait! He declared that "the Earth still requires some blood before it is ready to move into new and different areas."[6] He continued:

> The Guards of the Ancient era...the one dying right now...are not willing to give up their authority so easily. I foresee, on a mass scale, that the New Age is not going to come into being as so many people believe and wish to believe. I see it requiring a heck of a lot of blood, disruption, chaos, and pain for a mass change to occur.[7]

Have you guessed yet just who these "unfit" and "ignorant" people are? New Age propagandist John Randolf Price has declared that the unfit includes "any individual or group who denies the divinity of man.[8] That narrows it down some doesn't it? Price has also been in conversation with his "entity" who goes by the name of Asher. This "entity" tells Price that the New Age shall establish universal peace, and protect all of the world's three billion inhabitants. Price says, "But you've only covered slightly more than half of the world's population. What about the others?"[9] Asher replies:

> Nature will soon enter her cleansing cycle. Those who reject the earth changes with an

attitude of "it can't happen here" will
experience the greatest emotion of fear and
panic, followed by rage and violent action.
These individuals, with their lower vibration
rates, will be removed during the next two
decades.[10]

Price tells Asher that "wiping out more than two billion
people off the face of the earth is a little drastic, don't you
think?"[11] The "entity" answers by saying, "who are we to say
that those people did not volunteer to be a part of the destruction . . . Never forget that each individual has free will and
free choice." This is true, Maitreya cannot "force" Christians
to worship him; but when we don't, we are "volunteering"
ourselves to go into the spirit realm. New Age spokesman Ken
Eyers says that "Those who cannot be enlightened will not be
permitted to dwell in this world. They will be sent to some
equally appropriate place to work their way to understanding."

David Spangler, a New Age leader, has confided that those
sent to the spiritual will "be contained and ministered to until
such a time as they can be safely released into physical
embodiment again.[12] All of this shouldn't surprise us, as far
back as the last century men like British Socialist Harold Laski
have declared, "Sterilize all the unfit, among whom I include
all fundamentalists."[13] This sentiment was echoed by the
Nazis, who declared, "As society progresses in a spiral, we
will again come to see the higher morality of destroying
the unfit."[14]

The Bible warns Christians of the tribulation: a time when
the Antichrist shall appear and a holocaust shall commence.
The Jews have already had their holocaust. Six million Jews,
innocent men, women, and children, were tortured and murdered in the Nazi death camps. During the closing months of
the war, when fuel and trains were worth their weight in gold
to the German Army, Hitler ordered them to be used for the
transportation of more Jews to the death camps. Why?
Because, we must understand, the propaganda about bringing
world peace and a master race was just that: propaganda.

Hitler's real aim was the destruction of the Jews. In every land he conquered the first thing he ordered was the rounding up and transportation of the Jews to the death camps. Remember, Hitler said that Jewish blood would contaminate the pure Aryan stock in the new world that he and his Nazi chiefs were building.

Ghulam said he was sent to "kill the swine." He often referred to Christians as ants, dung, and, of course, pigs. He addressed his own followers differently. His words to them were soft, even flattering. He always addressed them as, "O my friends, O my dear ones"[15]

Hitler killed the Jews because they "hindered" Aryanism. Alice Bailey taught that the Jews were killed because they had "bad national karma." New Age propagandist Timothy Leary (who "turned-on" an entire generation to drugs back in the late 60s and early 70s) is now travelling to college campuses blaming the world's ills on guess who:

> Many problems we face today are caused by fundamentalist religion-Middle East crises, the current war-like atmosphere based on fanaticism—people who totally believe in their own cause....This is the familiar position taken by...the right wing Christian, etc.[16]

Fundamentalist Christians are an affront to Lucifer and his hosts, including his human hosts. New Age propagandists tell their followers only in thinly veiled hints that the "Christians must go." Once Maitreya is in power, the hints will become more bold. We are seen as ignorant, superstitious, dangerous fanatics whose "bad karma" is preventing this earth from its next quantum leap in evolution.

We will be given a chance to change, to worship Maitreya like the rest of the world. New Ager, Barbara Hubbard, says, "People will either change or die. That is the choice."[17] New Age propagandists now tell the uninitiated New Ager that he is a partner in bringing about world peace and universal brotherhood to all. Yet, there is a growing number of initiated

New Agers, who know a "higher" level of this truth. They are told that this millennium of peace will come, but not without breaking a few eggs.

The Third Reich was an empire dedicated to the genocide of world Jewry. Will the new Ottoman empire, the New World Order, be there for the sole purpose of the ultimate destruction of the Christians? How will the New World Order take power—Benjamin Creme comments:

> At the head of several of the governments of the world and in the great world agencies, like the United Nations' agencies, there will be either a Master or at least a third degree Initiate. So the great international agencies will be under the direct control of a high member of the Hierarchy. The Christ will be, not distant from humanity but the leader. He will show the way, outline the possibilities, outline the Plan. He will be the World Teacher....The Christ Himself will have a great deal to do—with the release of energies; the work of Initiation, as the Initiator, the Hierophant, at the first two Initiations; and stimulating and inspiring the formation of the New World Religion.[18]

Maitreya is to lead the New World Order which is to be a synthesis of the New World State and the New World Religion. The various United Nations agencies (directed now by Theosophist Robert Muller) are to prepare the way. What does Creme mean by the "release of energies"? He states further that the United Nations agencies will create an international trust, so that "no country owns anything." The "energy" shall also be "in trust" to the United Nations. Creme says, "The Masters [shall] have custodianship of scientific knowledge....the knowledge of means of power, nuclear power, simple and safe, which would answer the energy demands of all mankind. That is the crux of the situation today. It all has to do with energy. Whoever has the energy today has the power."

Creme says that this nuclear energy shall be "shared" with all nations under the "trusteeship" of the U.N. of course. In other words, nuclear power is too dangerous for opposing ideologies (the Americans and their allies and the Soviets and their allies) to control. There must be a "Third Force" that will be neutral, peaceful, sharing, and will control the nuclear power so that the world doesn't explode.

Like the Jews, fundamentalists and Evangelical Christians exist in every nation in the world. The New World Order would have to be just that—international, if they were to gather the Christians for a free trip to spirit realms. If the United Nations, controlled by the New Group of World Servers, had control of all the nuclear arsenal, then it could force every nation to "deliver up" the Christians. Many professing Christ will, no doubt, bend the knee to Baal. The true Evangelical and fundamentalist Christians will be fewer than what is counted now—the threat of death will assure that. Those that do not receive the mark will be "marked" for extinction. Nations that refuse to deliver up the Christians will be threatened with nuclear annihilation.

Who will be the ruler of the New World Order? Creme and others say it will be Maitreya. He will come working miracles, and speaking of sharing and brotherly love. Yet, as soon as he is in power, the veil will come off. Blood will flow in the streets. Millions will starve from mismanagement. The Christians will be to blame. Then, it will happen.

If the evil entity that possessed Ghulam Ahmad is to possess another who is to work miracles, and deceive the nations, then when will this take place? We have seen that Maitreya has appeared publicly in Nairobi. The "main event" will be his "Day of Declaration" over world radio and television. When will that take place? Remember, the possession of Krishnamurti failed because the American masses weren't ready. This time the Masters will prepare America! In this next chapter, I will show how the Masters are preparing our nation for the Day of Declaration, and examine the

preparation New Age leaders and propagandists are making
now for the triumphant entry of their "Lord" Maitreya.

# 8.

# PART EIGHT

## The Luciferian Initiation

The Creme ad asks, "When will we see him?" The ad continues:

> He has not yet declared His true status, and His location is known to only a very few disciples. One of these has announced that soon the Christ will acknowledge His identity and within the next two months will speak to humanity through a worldwide television and radio broadcast. His message will be heard inwardly, telepathically, by all people in their own language. From that time, with His help, we will build a new world.

The two months came and went, but no Maitreya. Why? Creme said that it was the fault of the media: not enough coverage for such a great event. As I mention earlier, my sources reveal a different reason. Tahir Ahmad, the present head of the Ahmadiyya movement and Khalifat-ul-Masih IV, came to that position in June of 1982—two months after the ads came out.

According to my sources, Rahmat Ahmad was expected to become the Khalifat-ul-Masih in June 1982 because of Tahir's fading health. This did not happen. However, Rahmat's turn is coming soon. Once the next successor comes in office, he is to take upon himself the "spirit and power" of Ghulam.

During the last seventy years gurus and yogis have flocked to America. Why? To train a dedicated cadre. For what purpose? So that this cadre could initiate the rest of us into the New Age: the Luciferic Initiation. They will do this very subtly, and most of us won't know that we're being initiated. A fundamentalist Christian America spelled defeat for the Masters, and ended the possession of Krishnamurti as the Great World Teacher. Another candidate for the job is now here, and the Masters want to make sure that the masses in America will receive this "Christ" with open arms.

What is the Luciferic Initiation? It is designed to transform our thinking. Once our thinking is transformed, then our actions will follow. It is designed to destroy all of God's institutions: the family, marriage, and this country. The plan for initiation is set, and being carried out now.

The American masses are being initiated into the New Age, and most of them don't even know it! New Age doctrines are being taught in veiled terms and in subtle and deceitful ways in every area of our society: education, politics, television, movies, business, and even so-called Christian churches. Why? For one reason only, so that we will all bend the knee to Baal (Sanat Kumara), his Baalim (the Masters of Wisdom), and his "Christ" (Maitreya). A full exposé of this widespread but subtle Luciferic Initiation is the subject of the second volume in this trilogy: Antichrist Conspiracy. For those who cannot wait, here are a few brief examples.

## *EDUCATION*

The United States spends more money on education than any nation in the world. We have more teachers with better training, equipment, and knowledge than any nation in the world. We have the technology that sent men to the moon and live moving pictures back for the world to see. If we're such an advanced nation, then why are so many of our high school graduates leaving school without the ability to read an application for employment? Could it be that this is part of the plan.

New Age propagandist Paul Blanchard may have the answer. He wrote, "I think that the most important factor in moving us toward a secular society has been the educational factor. Our schools may not teach Johnny how to read properly, but the fact that Johnny is in school until he is sixteen tends to lead toward the elimination of religious superstition. The average American child now acquires a high school education, and this militates against Adam and Eve and all other myths of alleged history." In an article called "A Religion for a New Age," another New Age/Humanist propagandist wrote:

> The battle for humankind's future must be waged and won in the public school classroom by teachers who correctly perceive their role as proselytizers of a new faith; a religion of humanity that recognizes and respects the spark of what theologians call divinity in every human being. These teachers must embody the same selfless dedication as the most rabid fundamentalist preachers, for they will be ministers of another sort, utilizing a classroom instead of a pulpit to convey humanist values in whatever subject they teach, regardless of the educational level ... The classroom must and will become an arena of conflict between the old and the new—the rotting corpse of Christianity, together with all its adjacent evils and misery, and the new faith of humanism...

A generation ago children learned the "Three R's": reading, writing, and arithmetic. Supplementing these skills was Bible study—so that the child would grow with a strong moral conviction. Today, however, the curriculum is changing. In

many schools students spend a fair amount of their days
studying "value clarifications." They are being taught "alternative lifestyles." They are being instructed on how to use the
schools clinic—a place where one can get information on
condoms, abortion, and "safe" sex. This is only the beginning,
the Education Network for the Association of Humanistic
Psychology, which has an immense say on what schools
ultimately teach, gives us some insight on what's coming next:

> The students will: do yoga each morning
> before class; interpret their astrological charts;
> send messages via ESP; mind project; astral
> project; heal their own illness; speak with their
> "Higher Selves" and receive information
> necessary for joyful living; lift energies from
> the power chakra to the heart chakra; practice
> skills necessary for color healing; hold an
> image of themselves as being perfect; receive
> advice from their personal guides; merge
> minds with others in the class to experience the
> collective consciousness of the group.

Impossible? If a Christian dared even to suggest his
religion in class he would be fired, ostracized, and probably
sued by the ACLU. However, as early as ten years ago, *Time*
magazine reported one Professor David Weltha who taught
public university courses in ESP, Astrology, and reincarnation. The article states that Weltha offers a course as
University Studies 313G, "Your Former Lives." When a few
brave souls objected they were quickly silenced. When
reporters asked the university's chief of academic affairs
about the course, and why it should be taught in a public
school, he replied, "It's the sort of thing that keeps a university
lively."

The New Ager will say, "Ah, but the Bible is taught as
literature in public schools, why not our beliefs?" Wrong. The
Bible is not taught in public schools. The "Bible as Literature"
courses should be renamed "The Bible is Only Literature!"
They are taught by Liberal "Christian" professors that attempt

to ruin the listeners' faith. We shall see in detail the deception and open violations of scholarly method by liberal Bible professors in Antichrist conspiracy.

Yes, they are using public schools to degrade the Bible, deride Christianity, teach "alternative" lifestyles (which the Bible calls "abominations"), and to initiate the unwary students into the New Age. The U.S. wasn't ready for Krishnamurti, but it will be ready for Maitreya. All with your tax dollars.

How are the problems of the world to be solved? Car education play a role. Gorbachev has suggested that, "A world consultative council under the U.N. auspices uniting the world's intellectual elite would be globally beneficial." What do you know, this already exists: it is called The New Group of World Servers! Is this a coincidence?

## *TELEVISION*

In this country, the television has become the dominant form of communication. It has also become the "electronic parent" for our children. This is what Esteves Roland had to say about this problem in his article in *Marriage and Family Living* magazine:

> Preschoolers spend more time watching TV than it takes to earn a college degree. By the time of high school graduation, most children will have sat only 11,000 [hours] in school, but more than 15,000 hours in front of the television. Only about one-third of all parents attempt to control the amount and content of
>
> television their children watch. Television has the power to enhance or stunt the child's growth.

The power of television is inconceivable. The author of the book *Subliminal Suggestion* has written: "The TV machine regulates time, channelizes or unifies perceptual experience and establishes (all subliminally) an entire range

of human expectations, value systems, identities, relationships, and perspectives toward the entire world . . . [IT] holds
such a devastating potential for brainwashing, mass
programming, and the destruction of individualism . . ."

What are our children watching on television? Let's see a
few examples. Saturday morning cartoons are never missed
by most children. A generation ago children watched
humorous pigs, rabbits, ducks, mice, and road-runners. These
cartoons even taught moral values. Daffy Duck was always
shown to be the fool when he got too greedy or deceptive.
Now things have changed. Children's cartoons, and games,
are fraught with occult imagery and doctrine. Here are just a
few examples:

· He-Man and the Masters of the Universe—He-Man is a
   blonde Aryan God-man. He and his cohorts are battling
   the forces of Darkness. The cartoon includes pyramidology, crystal power, serpents, ram-heads, and other occult
   imagery.

· She-Ra, Princess of Power—She-Ra is just a backwards
   name for Ra-Maat. She is Maat. She-Ra fights the forces
   of darkness while riding her unicorn (New Age symbol).

. The Smurfs—Papa Smurf is a witch doctor who casts
   spells and makes potions. Occult symbolism appears in
   almost every show.

A New Age magazine, *Shaman's Drum*, discusses these
cartoons, here, specifically, The Ewoks:

> Every Saturday morning millions of kids of all
> ages are treated to lessons in shamanic practice
> on the "Ewoks" cartoon show, produced by
> George Lucas of *Star Wars* and *Raiders of the
> Lost Ark* fame. Nearly every show involves
> good Ewok shaman Logray doing battle with
> his arch enemy Morag, and the word shaman

is used directly. Clairvoyant dreams, talking trees, magical spells, amulets, and wisdom teachings are gently woven into this entertaining and popular series.

In cartoons, we are increasingly seeing the "good" wizard, or witch, in battle with the "bad" wizards, or witches. Of course, the children aren't told just "who" these bad and evil forces are. They learn that in school. What is it? The racist, sexist, imperialistic, Judeo-Christian ("Old Age") society.

Television is preparing adults as well. The news media is overwhelmingly liberal/New Age. Practically within the same breath, the newscaster will tell about fundamentalist terrorists kidnapping people, and then fundamentalist marching on Washington.

Probably the most-watched television series in recent years was Carl Sagan's "Cosmos." Sagan remarked that, "The cosmos is all that is, or ever was, or ever will be." In the series, Sagan indoctrinated the viewers by proclaiming that evolution was fact, not theory (actually, it's fiction), and offered thinly veiled praises of Hinduism. What does Sagan (who is a leading New Age propagandist) suggest? He declares, "If we must worship a power greater than ourselves, does it not make sense to revere the sun and stars?"

Another television mini-series that broke records was Shirley MacLain's "Out on a Limb." What does she preach over prime time family viewing? Astrology, reincarnation, yoga, etc. Her book, by the same name, became a runaway best-seller. In it she wrote, "The tragedy of the human race was that we had forgotten we were all Divine." I haven't even mentioned the mountain of sex, violence, and deviant behavior promoted by the major networks in their programing. America's viewing audience is being programmed. New Age philosophy promoted by the media insures that Maitreya will be welcome when he arrives.

New Age doctrine has invaded the cinema. George Lucas, creator of the *Star Wars* saga with Irvin Kershner, has publicly admitted that the films are rife with Zen Buddhism.  What is Zen Buddhism? Alan Watts, a former "Liberal" Episcopalian priest, now a Zen Master, has said that, "The appeal of Zen, as of the Eastern philosophy, is that it unveils ... a vast region where at last the self is indistinguishable from God."

George Lucas has declared that, "There is a God and there is both a good side and a bad side.  You have a choice between them, but it works better if you're on the good side." Initiates know that the dark side of the "Force" is Satan, and the good side is "Lucifer" (some choice eh?).

Another popular film has been *2001: A Space Odyssey*. It created quite a stir when it first came out in 1970.  It wasn't until recently that movie goers learned the secret of the monolith.  In *2010*, the sequel to *2001*, and brain-child of New Age propagandist Arthor C. Clarke, the monoliths reproduce like antibodies, and cave-in on Jupiter.  What happens? Jupiter becomes a new sun.  World problems of overpopulation and hunger are "cured" because the growing seasons are doubled, and people may now populate Jupiter's moons. What is Jupiter's new name?  They call it Lucifer!

Another New Age film that has shaken the cinemas is *The Last Temptation of Christ*.  Here are a few quotes from the film: Jesus says to Mary Magdalene: "I've done a lot of wrong things." To a group of poor, sick people who came to him for healing he says, "Get away, you sicken me; you're selfish and full of hate." The movie portrays Jesus marrying Mary Magdelene.  An angel wants to watch while Jesus and Mary have sex.  The angels says, "I wondered if I could watch—I'm lonely too," Jesus laughs and responds, "Yes, yes, watch."

It is interesting to note that when Christianity is being presented, it is presented as the "religion" of the Ku Klux Klan or as a religion of ignorant simpletons: harmless (if left out of politics and government), but not for the thinking audience (which every viewer believes he or she is).

Steven Speilberg has been another of the giants in the movie industry.  His top money-making hits preach straight

New Age doctrine. In his movie *Poltergeist*, Speilberg tells the story of a middle-class family who is terrorized by a terrible entity call the "Beast." Only a psychic can help them, and only if they go against their "Christian" upbringing. They do, and the psychic helps them recover their daughter whom the "Beast" has kidnapped. In *Poltergeist II* we discover just who the "Beast" is. A fundamentalist Christian preacher long dead! In the sequel the preacher enters the man—who then tries to rape his wife. Family entertainment? This time an Indian Shaman (witch doctor) is called in, and, again, they are successful. The deception continues.

## BUSINESS

The New Age is everywhere in the business world. Drugs, embezzlement, and related problems are causing America's businesses to lose hundreds of billions a year. To "solve" these problems (that occultism has created), the New Age has come to the rescue like a knight in shining armor.

New Age propagandists are telling corporations that these problems can be solved when employees' minds are transformed (called by other names, of course). Major companies are spending "about 4 billion " in corporate dollars each year on New Age self-improvement and self-motivational programs.43 Many of these programs, which feature thinly veiled instruction in yoga, psychic powers, etc., are mandatory for employees. When Christians ask not to participate in such things, they are often "asked" to leave the company.

The New Age has also crept into the areas of music, literature, and all other areas of society. America is being prepared, indoctrinated, and brainwashed into the New Age. Why? So that we will open our arms wide for Maitreya and open our minds for his Masters of Wisdom to enter. The time is near!

## ACT NOW

In the next few years, Maitreya will announce his "Day of Declaration." Millions of devoted followers will bow to him and recognize him as the answer to all the world's problems. Undoubtedly, the Christian community will wonder if he is the Antichrist foretold in the Bible or just another one of many false messiahs. Either way, Christians should prepare themselves for the changes about to occur.

The anti-Christian mood in this country is already dangerously high. The similarities between Nazi Germany and the Jewish community in the 1920s and 1930s are all too obvious. A whole new generation is about to enter adulthood and step into positions of authority in this country. Our Judeo-Christian past has been ingeniously hidden from them by those who desire to remake America into a secular society.

The first amendment was written by our founders with the intention of protecting the Church from the state. Today, the very same amendment that was written to protect the Church from encroachment has been used to silence the Church. William Penn, the founder of Pennsylvania, once said, "we will be governed by God or ruled by tyrants." Unfortunately, we have rejected our Judeo-Christian past and are about to go the way of all nations that flout the laws of God, i.e., we will soon be ruled by tyrants.

The degree of anti-Christian sentiment can be felt at all societal levels. Zavala Elementary in Houston, Texas, recently removed books that they felt were outdated. What books were removed? "Several Stories of Jesus," "Jesus of Nazareth," "A Picture Dictionary of the Bible," "Thomas Jefferson and His World." Compare this to the books that were allowed to remain: a book on divorce, a book on witches, learning about witches, and books training children in values clarification.[1]

This doesn't mean we are hopelessly lost. It's not too late to turn the tide. If the Christian community will educate itself in order to recognize the New Age assault, it's not too late to act. The Church has been persecuted throughout history and managed to emerge as the head and not the tail. If Christians will awaken from their slumber and once again heed the advice of Christ to be the "salt of the earth," the gates of hell will not prevail.

## THE BIBLE CONDEMNS NEW AGE DOCTRINE

- Witchcraft (Deut. 1:10)
- Fortune-telling (Deut. 1:10)
- Communication with entities (Deut. 1:11)
- Channeling (Deut. 18:11)
- Astrology (Deut. 4:19, Gen. 3:5)
- Self-deification (Isa. 14:12, Gen. 3:5)
- Lying (John 8:44)
- Idolatry (1 Cor. 10:19-20)

# Notes

## PART ONE: A LOOK AT SEVERAL FALSE MESSIAHS THROUGHOUT HISTORY

1. *Encyclopedia Judaica*, Vol. 4, 228.
2. Ibid., 228.
3. Jack Gratus, *The False Messiahs* (New York: Taplinger Publishing, 1975), 55.
4. John Evelyn, *The History of the Three Late Famous Imposters* (London, 1669), 60.
5. Gershom G. Scholem, *Major Trends in Jewish Mysticism* (London: Thames & Hudson, 1955), 287-290.
6. Joseph Kastein, *The Messiah of Ismir, Sabbatai Zevi* (London: John Lane, 1931), 189.
7. Ibid., 151.
8. Norman Cohn, *The Pursuit of the Millennium* (London: Seeker & Warbug, 1957), 268.
9. Ibid.
10. Baring S. Gould, *Historical Oddities and Strange Events* (London: Methuen & Company, 1891), 301.
11. Ibid., 343.
12. E. Belfort Bax, *Rise and Fall of the Anabaptists* (London: Sonnenschein, 1903), 318-319.
13. Clifford Goldstein, "The Pantheon of Pretenders," *Liberty* (March/April 1986): 9-10.
14. Ibid.
15. Clara E. Sears, *Days of Delusion* (Boston and New York: Houghton Mufflin Co., 1916), 68.
16. Hannah Smith, *Religious Fanaticism* (London: Faber & Gwyer, 1928), 48.
17. Abba H. Silver, *A History of Messianic Speculation* (New York: Macmillian Co., 1927), 58.
18. Dave Hunt, *The Cult Explosion* (Eugene, OR: Harvest House Publishing, 1978), 221.
19. Clifford Goldstein, "Antichrist," *Liberty* (May/June 1985): 25.
20. Joseph A. Seiss, *The Apocalypse* (Philadelphia: Approved Books, 1865), 82.
21. Martin Kiddle, *The Revelation of St. John* (New York: Harper and Brothers, 1936), 159.
22. Isbon T. Beckwith, *The Apocalypse of John* (New York: Macmillian Co., 1919), 563.
23. Thomas S. Kepler, *The Book of Revelation* (New York: Oxford University Press, 1957), 62.
24. Barbara Walker, *The Woman's Encyclopedia of Myths and Secrets* (San Francisco: Harper & Row, 1983), s.v. "Apollo-Python."
25. Flavius Philostratus, *The Life of Apollonius of Tyana*, trans. F.C. Conybeare (Cambridge, Mass.: Harvard University Press, 1960), 11-14.
26. Ibid., 253.
27. *The New Schaff-Herzog Religious Encyclopedia* (Grand Rapids, MI.: Baker Book House, 1977), s.v. "Apollonius of Tyana."
28. Alexander Hislop, *The Two Babylons* (New York: Loizeaux Brothers Publishers, 1943), 278-279.
29. Richard Cavendish, *Man, Myth, and Magic* (New York: Cavendish, 1970), 1629.
30. Flavius Philostratus, *The Life of Apollonius of Tyana*, trans. F.C. Conybeare (Cambridge, Mass.: Harvard University Press, 1960), 13-15.
31. Flavius Philostratus, *The Life and Times of Apollonius of Tyana*, trans. Charles Ells (Palo Alto, CA.: Stanford University Press, 1923), 10.
32. Philostratus, *Apollonius of Tyana*, trans. Conybeare, ch. 31.
33. Philostotus, *Apollonius of Tyana*, trans. Conybeare, 317.
34. Ibid., 9.
35. Ibid., 447.
36. Alexander Hislop, *The Two Babylons* (New York: Loizeaux Brothers Publishers, 1943), 269-270.
37. Ibid., 87.
38. Ibid., 278.
39. J.M. Robertson, *Pagan Christ* (New Hyde Park, New York: University Books, 1967), 96-97.
40. G.R.S. Mead, *Apollonius of Tyana* (New Hyde Park, New York: Uni-

versity Books, 1966), 5.

41. F.W. Groves Campbell, *Apollonius of Tyana* (Chicago: Argonaut Publishers, 1968), 9-10.

42. Mead, *Apollonius of Tyana*, 5.

43. F.C. Conybeare, *The Origins of Christianity* (New York: University Books, 1958), 143.

44. Gerhard Uhlhorn, *The Conflict of Christianity with Heathenism* (New York: Charles Scribner's Sons, 1879), 331-333.

## PART TWO: WHAT DO WE KNOW ABOUT LORD MAITREYA?

1. Benjamin Creme, *The Reappearance of the Christ and the Masters of Wisdom* (London: Tara Press, 1980), 14.

2. Ibid., 15.

3. Ibid., 46.

4. Ibid., 53-54.

5. Ibid., 30.

6. Ibid., 25-26.

7. Ibid., 49.

8. Ibid., 55.

9. Ibid., 94.

10. Ibid., 140.

11. Ibid., 78.

12. Ibid., 71.

13. Benjamin Creme, *Messages from Maitreya the Christ*, Vol. 1 (London: Tara Press, 1980), 16-17.

14. Creme, *Reappearance of the Christ*, 222.

15. Ibid., 69.

16. Ibid., 76.

17. Ibid., 88.

18. Ibid., 89.

19. Ibid.

20. Ibid., 115.

21. G.H. Lang, *World Chaos* (London: Praternoster Press, 1948), 16.

22. Ibid., 17.

## PART THREE—THE OLD AGE IS DECAYING

1. "The Tower of Babel," *Magical Blend* 15(1987): 1.

2. "The Power of One," *Life Times* (winter 86/87): 84.

3. John Randolph Price, *The Planetary Commission* (Austin, TX.: Quartus Books, 1984), 32.

4. Kimberly French, "Finding a Drop to Drink," *Whole Life Times* (July/August 1982).

5. Lowell Ponte, "Food: America's Secret Weapon," *Reader's Digest* (May 1982): 66.

6. Ibid., 67.

7. Ibid., 67-68.

8. Tom Anderson, "Food for War," *American Opinion* (May 1969): 29-30.

9. Yonas Deressa, "Rebel Aid," *National Review* (April 24, 1987): 36.

10. Bob Phillips, *When the Earth Quakes* (Wheaton, IL.: Key Publishers, 1973), 20.

11. John Campbell Oman, *The Brahmans, Theists, and Muslims of India* (Delhi, India: Indological Book House, n.d.), 37.

12. Maureen Stafford and Dora Ware, *An Illustrated Dictionary of Ornamentation* (New York: St. Marrin's Press, 1974), s.v. "Triquetrum."

13. Alice L. Hageman, ed., *Sexist Religion and Women in the Church* (New York: Association Press, 1974), 125.

14. Ibid., 137.

15. Denise Lardner Carmody, *Women and World Religions* (Nashville: Abingdon Press, 1979), 45-46.

16. Ibid., 51.

17. Ibid., 50.

18. Carmody, *Women and World Religions*, 114-115.

19. Joseph J. Carr, *The Twisted Cross* (Lafayette, LA.: Huntington House Publishers, 1985), 87.

20. Ibid., 276.

21. Dave Hunt, *Peace Prosperity, and the Coming Holocaust* (Eugene, OR.: Harvest House Publishers, 1983), 151.

22. Henry S. Lucas, *The Renaissance and the Reformation* (New York: Harper and Row Publishers, 1934), 136.

# PART FOUR: PREPARING THE PUBLIC FOR LORD MAITREYA

1. *Golden Book of the Theosophical Society* (Adyar, India: Theosophical Publishing Trust, 1925), 63.
2. John Symonds, *Madame Blavatsky, Medium and Magician* (New York, 1960), 287.
3. Ibid.
4. Ibid.
5. Ibid.
6. Gregory Tillett, *The Elder Brother* (London: Routledge and Kegan Paul, 1982), 51.
7. Mary Lutysen, *Krishnamurti: The Years of Awakening* (London, 1957), 35.
8. Tillett, *The Elder Brother,* 149.
9. Ibid., 149-150.
10. Ibid., 280.
11. Ibid., 153.
12. H. Blavatsky, "What's in a Name," *Lucifer* (September 15, 1887): 2.
13. Tillett, *The Elder Brother,* 131-132.
14. Charles W. Ferguson, *The Confusion of Tongues* (Grand Rapids, MI.: Zondervan Publishing House, 1936), 155.
15. Dave Hunt, *Peace, Prosperity, and the Coming Holocaust* (Eugene, OR.: Harvest House Publishers, 1983), 126.
16. Norman Geisler, *False Gods of Our Time* (Eugene, OR.: Harvest House, 1986), 34-35.

# PART FIVE: HOW WILL WE RECOGNIZE MAITREYA?

1. Henry James Forman, *The Story of Prophecy* (New York: Tudor Publishing Company, 1936), 328.
2. Ibid., 329.
3. J. Gordon Melton, *The Encyclopedia of American Religions* (Detroit, MI.: Gale Research Company, 1987), 60-61.
4. Constance Cumbey, *The Hidden Dangers of the Rainbow* (Lafayette, LA.: Huntington House Publishers, 1983), 67.
5. Norman Geisler, *False Gods of Our Time* (Eugene, Oregon: Harvest House, n.d.), 105.
6. Cumbey, *Hidden Dangers,* 19-20.
7. Texe Marrs, *Dark Secrets of the New Age* (Westchester, IL.: Crossway Books, 1987), 57-58.
8. Hal Lindsey, *The Late Great Planet Earth* (Grand Rapids, MI.: Zondervan Publishing House, 1970), 100-101.
9. B. de W. Weldon, *The Evolution of Israel* (London: Harrison and Sons, n.d.), 257-258, 299-301.
10. Benjamin Creme, *The Reappearance of the Christ and the Masters of Wisdom* (London: Tara Press, 1980), 33.
11. Ibid., 46.
12. Ibid., 69-70.
13. Ibid., 101.
14. Ibid., 180-181.
15. Ibid., 182.
16. Ibid., 190.
17. Ibid., 28.
18. N.W. Hutchings, "Is Maitreya the Anti-Christ," *The Gospel Truth* (July 1982): 1-2.
19. Ibid., 4.
20. The Christian Research Institute, "Benjamin Creme and the Reappearance of the Christ," *Forward*: 4.
21. Ibid., 3.
22. Marrs, *Dark Secrets,* 61.
23. Benjamin Creme, *Maitreya's Mission* (Amsterdam, Netherlands: Share International Foundation, 1986), 3.
24. Ibid.
25. Ibid., 3-4.
26. Ibid., 21.
27. Ibid., 12.
28. Ibid., 23.
29. Ibid., 27.
30. Ibid., 29.
31. Ibid., 5.
32. Ibid., 21.
33. Uriah Smith, *Thoughts, Critical and Practical, on the Book of Revelation* (Battle Creek, MI.: Seventh-day Adventist Publishing Association, 1885), 211-212.
34. David Reed, "Qaddafi: Libya's Lord of Terror," *Reader's Digest* (June

1981): 107.

35. Cumbey, *Hidden Dangers*, 90.

36. Martin Lings, "Sufis," *Man, Myth, and Magic*: 2714.

37. Ibid., 1469.

38. U. Ali, *Mohammed in Ancient Scriptures* (Agra, India: S.R. and Brothers, 1936), 1-2.

39. Ibid., 2.

40. Jean Dixon, *My Life and Prophecies* (New York: William Morrow and Company, 1969), 187.

41. Omar V. Garrison, *The Encyclopedia of Prophecy* (Secaucus, New York: Atadel Press, 1978), 26-27.

42. Rene Pache, *The Return of Jesus Christ* (Chicago: Moody Press, 1955), 193.

## PART SIX: WHAT IS LORD MAITREYA'S NAME?

1. Texe Marrs, *Mystery Mark of the New Age* (Westchester, IL.: Crossway Books, 1988), 47.

2. Geoffry Ashe, *The Ancient Wisdom* (London: Macmilian Ltd., 1977), 162.

3. Robert F. Riggs, *The Apocalypse Unsealed* (New York: Philosophical Library, 1981), 171-172.

4. Ibid., 170.

5. Benjamin Creme, *The Reappearance of the Christ and the Masters of Wisdom* (London: Tara Press, 1980), 46.

6. Edward Rice, *Eastern Definitions* (New York: Doubleday/Anchor Books, 1980), 398,400.

7. Marrs, *Dark Secrets*, 89.

## PART SEVEN: THE TEACHINGS OF MAITREYA (RAHMAT AHMAD)

1. Texe Marrs, *Dark Secrets of the New Age* (Westchester, IL.: Crossway Books, 1987), 208.

2. Maharishi Mahesh Yogi, *Inauguration of the Dawn of the Age of Enlightenment* (Fairfield, Iowa: Maharishi Int. University Press, 1975), 47.

3. Ruth Montgomery, *Threshold to Tomorrow* (New York: Ballantine/Fawcett Crest, 1982), 196.

4. Ibid., 196, 207.

5. Montgomery, *Threshold to Tomorrow*, 206-207.

6. Christopher Hyatt, "Undoing Yourself," *Magical Blend* 16 (1987): 22.

7. Ibid.

8. John Randolf Price, *The Planetary Commission* (Austin, TX.: Quartus Books, 1984), 163.

9. John Randolf Price, *Practical Spirituality* (Austin, TX.: Quartus Books, 1985), 21.

10. Ibid.

11. Ibid.

12. David Spangler, *Revelation: The Birth of a New Age* (Middleton, WI.: Lorian Press, 1975), 164.

13. Allan Chase, *The Legacy of Malthus* (New York: Alfred E. Knopy, 1977), 316.

14. Karl Binding, *Permitting the Destruction of Unworthy Life* (Germany, 1920).

15. Barakat Ahmad Rajeke, *Ahmadiyya Movement in India* (Qudian, India: Jai Hind Press, 1968), 24-25.

16. Timothy Leary, *Magical Blend* 13(1987).

17. Barbara Marx Hubbard, *Happy Birth Day Planet Earth* (Sante Fe, N.M.: Ocean Tree Books, 1986), 32.

18. Benjamin Creme, *The Reappearance of the Christ and the Masters of Wisdom* (London: Tara Press, 1980), 169.

## PART EIGHT: THE LUCIFERIAN INITIATION

1. Pat Robertson, *The Rising Storm* (June 1990): 3.

# Advertisement
## Introducing The *World Crusade Journal*

> Go ye therefore, and teach all nations . . . even
> unto the end of the world.
> (The Great Commission)

In this country alone there are thirty million cultists, sixty million occultists, and fifteen million who adhere to one of the World Religions. And I'm not counting the Humanists, whether secular or so-called religious. How are we, as born-again believers, going to take the Gospel to the ends of the earth when we can't even take care of this country? Something needs to be done.

The Cults are growing at alarming rates: Mormonism, Russellism (Jehovah's Witnesses, etc.), and even the lesser cults, such as Armstrongism, are growing so fast that they can't build churches fast enough to house their converts. It seems like the only time Christians want to witness to them is when a few of them wind up on their doorstep. The "witness" is usually a curt statement and a door slam, or, if not that, it's someone saying: "No thank you, we're Christians!" Then, the cultists just move on to someone else. Something needs to be done.

The occult is growing by leaps and bounds. The term "occult" comes from Latin: it means "hidden" or "secret." Under this category falls the New Age movement, and

Satanism. I like to call them the "light" and "dark" sides of the *force*. The "force" of course is Lucifer, who can change his normal evil appearance (Satanism) into an angel of light (the New Age).

In the U.S. alone there are about sixty million people who adhere to New Age doctrine and practices. While Christians can be jailed, or sued, or fired, for praying at school, New Age doctrine and practices have now become standard at many universities, high schools, and even elementary schools— Yoga for Health, visualization classes, evolution as fact, etc.

While getting a sermon in a secular paper, or getting Christian values in government is considered a "violation of the separation of Church and State," New Age doctrines and practices—under thinly veiled packages—are being actively and enthusiastically promoted in the secular press, and in government: the horoscope columns in newspapers, and the euthanasia bills in government, etc. Something needs to be done.

The world religions are no longer part of the "rest" of the world. In this country, there are now more Muslims than Jews. The religion of Buddhism is being embraced by millions with Hollywood leading the way.

In this country there are over half-a-million Sihks, most of them converts, and almost that many Bahaist. Islam is now the fastest growing religion in the world. Tens of thousands— soon hundreds of thousands—of Americans, mostly African Americans, are converting to Islam every year. We are supposed to bring the Gospel of the Cross to the world, but it seems as if the world is breaking the Cross in our own *front* yard! Something needs to be done.

Something has been done! I would like to introduce you to the *World Crusade Journal*. This new publication is dedicated to training Christians in taking "The Great Commission" to the cults, occult, and world religions. *The World Crusade Journal* is the official publication of *The Society for the Propagation & Revival of the Gospel, Incorporated*. You can call us the S.P.R.G. We are named after the first Protestant missionary society: The Society for the Propagation of the Gospel in Foreign Parts (SPG).

## ACCOUNT OF THE S.P.R.G.

After the "Maitreya no show" of 1982, I left the New Age on a spiritual quest. I spent two-years, full-time, studying the various religions of the world. I studied, deeply, everything from the Ahmadiyyah Movement in Islam to Zen Buddhism. I discovered, to my surprise, that Evangelical Christianity was the only system consistent with the observable facts. After my intellectual conversion, I had a born-again experience.

I wanted to take the knowledge that I had, on the New Age and world religions, and do some good with it. At that time I visited a number of Christian counter-cult ministries. I found them to be extremely well informed.

Yet, their weakness seemed to be in the area of evangelism. They were well prepared to "warn" Christians against the cults, occult, and world religions, but they seemed not to be concerned that much with training believers in seeking out and evangelizing non-believers. I wanted to find ways in which Christians could be trained—in their own churches—to find and witness to non-believers.

Some ministries I found were so caustic toward the religion that they were trying to "witness" to, that they succeeded, more often than not, in turning off the people they were trying to reach. Other ministries used such scholarly language that the common man could not understand what they were trying to say. Some seemed more concerned with "I'm gonna prove you wrong" than "You need Jesus in your life!" I felt that something needed to be done.

During my research, I found information on the S.P.G. Every trial and error imaginable was propagated. The culmination of three centuries, and the experiences of thousands of missionaries and evangelists to hundreds of different religions was at my feet. I spent thousands of hours studying this material, and I saw that there were certain *keys* to reaching the cults, occult, and world religions. I learned them. "Why reinvent the wheel" I said to myself.

I discovered that what worked with a Hindu would not work with a Muslim, and what worked with a Muslim would not work with a Mormon. After learning these *keys to evangelism*, I tried them. *They worked*! And why shouldn't they? They were tried and tested over three centuries, and on five continents.

## THE CHRISTIAN HARVESTER PROGRAM

Taking the knowledge that I had gained, I developed the Christian Harvester Program (CHP). This is a basic training program that trains believers in these *keys of evangelism*. The keys are basic, simple, and, above all, they work. To promote the CHP we formed The Society for the Propagation & Revival of the Gospel, Incorporated (S.P.R.G. Inc.).

# WORLD CRUSADE JOURNAL

Here are just a few of the Special Reports from the *World Crusade Journal*:

* The TRUTH About Evolution
* The Abortion Holocaust
* Witnessing To Jehovah's Witnesses
* The Perils of Pornography
* The Illuminati: Then & Now
* UFO: Friend or Foe?

These are from our upcoming *New Age Cults* series:

* Alliester Crowley & A.M.O.R.C.
* What the Heck is Eck?
* Mahikari of America

We will also be offering cassette tapes through the *World Crusade Journal*.

The *World Crusade Journal* solicits articles, research, and news clippings on the cults, occult (New Age etc.) World Religions, and other important issues facing Christians today.

The *World Crusade Journal* subscription rate is $12.00 for one year (6 issues),

Address *all* correspondence to:

S.P.R.G. Inc.
Box 9535
Tacoma, WA 98409

All donations to the S.P.R.G. Inc. are tax deductible. (see other side)

## SUBSCRIBE TODAY TO THE . . .
## WORLD CRUSADE
## JOURNAL

For your subscription to the *World Crusade Journal*, please 1) Fill-in the lines below, 2) carefully tear-out this page, 3) enclose this page in a stamped envelope, and mail it to S.P.R.G. Inc., P.O. Box 9535, Tacoma, WA 98409. We would appreciate any financial support to our ministry; that support will allow us to continue bringing the Gospel of Jesus to New Agers across the nation. Please remember to make-out your donation (by check or money order) to S.P.R.G. Inc.

### Please Print:

Name_____

Address _____

City State Zip Code _____

### (Check One or More)

___ Yes, please send me the first issue of my World Crusade Journal subscription. ($12.00 for one year [6 issues])

___ Yes, I would like to become a co-laborer with the S.P.R.G.

The Society for the Propagation and Revival of the Gospel, Incorporated, is a non-profit evangelistic organization committed to taking "The Great Commission" to the cults, occult, and world religions.